John B. Foley Jr.

Presence and Immortality

Presence and Immortality

by Gabriel Marcel

DUQUESNE UNIVERSITY PRESS, Pittsburgh, Pa.

Editions E. Nauwelaerts, Louvain

This book has been translated by
Michael A. Machado
and revised by
Henry J. Koren

This work was originally published
in a French edition by
Flammarion & Cie
Paris

Contents

Author's Preface   7
My Fundamental Purpose (1937)   11
Metaphysical Journal (1938)   31
Metaphysical Journal (1939)   43
Metaphysical Journal (1940)   51
Metaphysical Journal (1941)   67
Metaphysical Journal (1942)   73
Metaphysical Journal (1943)   91
Presence and Immortality (1951)   227
The Unfathomable An Unfinished Play (March,
     1919)   245

Author's Preface

The myth of Orpheus and Eurydice lies at the very heart of my existence.

It is surely not superfluous to introduce here some clarifications on the fundamental preoccupation which has predominated the composition of this book. We hope that it may express as clearly as possible the diverse yet closely knit aspects of a work which has been considered nearly always from a definite perspective rather than in its unity. It is also necessary to recognize that this unity as such is not easily accessible.

The greater part of this book is taken up with a diary which I kept in a somewhat intermittent manner, particularly in my house at Corrèze, during the second world war. This diary is a sequel to those which were published in 1927 (*The Metaphysical Journal*) and in 1934 (*Being and Having*, the first part).

Those who have seriously studied my thought know that approximately since the year 1925 I peremptorily gave up the idea of composing a systematic philosophical work. My thought has appeared to me more and more like a finding one's way, at times fraught with danger and marked by a certain amount of groping, some stops, some fresh beginnings and some questionings. When I published the *Metaphysical Journal*, I was far from being assured that it would find some readers. Experience has shown that my fears were without foundation and that, in widely different countries, there were persons ready to accompany me in what very much resembles a voyage of discovery.

Particularly since the end of the second world war, I was invited to give a number of lectures, not only in Europe, but in Lebanon, North Africa, Canada, South America and Japan. Each of these lectures can be considered as an attempt to focus on what was first presented to me in the form of the diary. Here the reader will find the text of two unpublished lectures: the first, dating from 1937 and prepared for the University of Ghent, has not been delivered to the public; the second, which dates from 1951, has been given in Rabat, in San Paolo and in some other South American cities. The content of the first is of an extremely general nature and seems suitable for acquainting the reader, not too familiar with my thought, with its main features. The second deals directly with the central problem which lies at the heart of this book: I have called it somewhere the Existential Premises of Immortality, the latter being considered in no way along the lines of traditional philosophy but in the perspective of the death of the other, the death of the being loved. It stands to reason moreover that this question is inseparable from a whole metaphysical context which clearly appears in the *Journal.*

But what could be legitimately a matter for surprise is that I have wished to include in this book a theatrical fragment written in 1919, one that has never been published until this time.

To begin with let me say that one can never be emphatic enough in showing the intimate link that unites philosophy and the theater in my work. On the other hand this first act of a play that was never finished takes on in my eyes a special importance: on reading it again at the end of December, 1958, I came to the conclusion that it would enrich and as it were substantiate the pages of the *Journal* which I had decided to publish. One will observe that the time in which this act takes place immediately follows the end of the first war, the very period in which I wrote it. It constitutes a testimony which at once reflects the mentality of the French of that period but which even more profoundly indicates the very great repercussion which the war had on my sensibility and on my thought, a repercussion which was undefined and which undoubtedly penetrated the innermost recesses of my being until the present time.

But there is much more. The scene between Edith and the Abbé Séveilhac is in my eyes one of the most significant that I have written. My conversion to the Catholic religion was to take place only some ten years later; but I must add that the anxious interrogation formulated by the young woman and, I must add, so misunderstood by the priest, still retains for me its entire value. Strangely enough there appears already in 1919, prior to the sorrows which were to darken my existence, the problem on the subject of which, some thirty years later, I had to take exception to against some Doctors of the Church in reference to Marcel de Jouvenel's book, *Le Diapason du Ciel* (*The Concert of Heaven*), to which I wrote the introduction. True, in *The Unfathomable*, there is no question of messages through automatic writing. But the question of communication between life and the after-life is posed in its essence as it had to be a little later in *The Iconoclast*, the first version of which, *The Sword-bearer*, had been written during the war in 1917, if I am not mistaken.

Some will perhaps be inclined to think that I could have been satisfied with reproducing the scene between Edith and the Abbé Séveilhac, while omitting those that precede it. It seems to me that this would be a mutilation which would not allow the readers to put the scene in its context and would not give it its full weight.

Should we regret that the play was not finished? On reflection I do not think so. As a friend said, after having understood this act, it literally leads to the edge of a cliff. This is what moreover gave me the idea of entitling it *The Unfathomable*. The titles envisaged in 1919 no longer satisfy me. By continuing the play as I had originally intended, I would have risked weakening this feeling of an abyss which seems to emerge from the scene, more precisely from the last two scenes.

The word "abyss" must here assume its full meaning. I think that one would radically misunderstand the true characteristics of my thought, such as it is expressed particularly in the *Journals* at Corrèze, if one did not understand that it is above all a travelling along a ridge above an abyss. This has remained true even after my conversion, for one has a really poor and caricatural idea of the Faith if one imagines it to be a kind of talisman or good-luck charm. Faith is life, a life in which joy and anguish continually jostle each other, a life which will remain to the end menaced by the only temptation against which in the last analysis we must guard ourselves, namely that of despair.

My Fundamental
Purpose (1937)

In attempting to disengage some essential themes of my philosophic thought, for the purpose of a lecture which I must give in Ghent within the coming month, I have come to recognize, in a way that has disconcerted even me somewhat, the extent of the difficulty in exposing this thought *ex cathedra*. This is due to a number of reasons on which I am bound to insist. I think it necessary to point out certain obstacles which anyone who claims to give a general idea of my work inevitably runs into.

The first difficulty, a comparatively superficial one, but the deep roots of which I shall have to lay bare, consists in this that my philosophic work does not really permit itself to be dissociated from my theatre. In fact, the latter in no way constitutes an illustration or a translation of a certain body of thoughts which would preexist and which would have been first presented in an abstract form. Actually, as the best interpreters of my thought have observed, the drama must be accorded a veritable primacy in my work. How often I have anticipated in my plays certain conclusions which I only arrived at later on the philosophic plane!

Nothing is more striking in this regard than the final scene of *The Iconoclast* in which the positive value of mystery is recognized.

However, someone may tell me: "Be that as it may, nothing prevents you from isolating these conclusions from the dramatic context in which they are originally found to be inserted and formulating them in their abstract purity." Here we must be careful: the most important, the most significant of my plays—*The Quartet, The Iconoclast, The Road from Crete*, and especially *The Hungry Hearts*—reach their *dénouement* in a complex accord, in a harmony in which the spectator, or the reader, is invited to participate, but which does not let itself be reduced to formulas without being altered in some degree. As one character in *The Quartet* says: "Shall this thought in which we shall be all alone die in the words?" It pertains to drama, as to music, to realize beyond discursive knowledge, properly so called, a superior awareness in which our being finds itself presented in its integrity and which transcends the abstract statements with which pure intelligence is obliged to be satisfied.

It is towards consonances of this order that my philosophic thought is oriented. It is essentially polyphonic and is thereby radically opposed to all the ideologies more or less directly issuing from the French philosophical thought of the eighteenth century.

Nay more, when I attempt to proceed with regard to my own writings, as I would if it were a matter of accounting for another's philosophy—and this seems to me not only a licit but also a commendable approach—I find myself confronted with serious difficulties.

When I turn to my early writings, I recognize in them, as it were transparently, the essential thoughts which I have been trying to express for the last ten years. The language is altogether different, however, and I cannot help asking myself if I am not arbitrarily projecting into them a meaning which these writings did not have at the time when I wrote them. Moreover, this tends to make me rather sceptical of the value of many of the works on the history of philosophy. Actually these works entail some reinterpretations and one cannot say precisely whether they are legitimate or not.

To be honest it would be possible for me to forget about these early writings altogether. But I must confess that my difficulty is more fundamental still. It will always be impossible for me, I imagine, to present anything which smacks of display or resembles some demonstration models, each of which corresponds to a theory more or less skilfully linked with associated theories. In fact, it does not seem to me that philosophical research entails, in the same sense that scientific investigation does, an acquisition which the mind does not question anew and from which it sets out in order to extend its conquests.

I am inclined to think that it is of the essence of a living philosophical thought always to question, in some degree, the conclusions which it has gradually arrived at, and this, I must insist, at the risk of appearing not only discouraging, but hopeless.

Many a time I happened to focus my attention on these two phrases: "my system" or "my philosophy," only to be appalled by their ludicrous character. This feeling has always expressed itself in the unbearable discomfort I experience when someone asks me—and these are generally society women—to state in a few words "in what consists my philosophy." This request is enough to annihilate any awareness that I might have of it. It seems to me that I have always felt, without perhaps formulating it for myself with such clarity, that by definition philosophy is not, and cannot be, anything that one holds on to, anything that one has. No philosopher worthy of the name has to my mind been able to apprehend his own doctrine as a prerogative or as a possession, unless it were in the course of polemics in which he saw it being challenged and in which he had to defend it as one defends one's life. But it would be necessary to ask oneself if, from the moment in which it is thus treated as a "having," a philosophy does not degrade itself, does not change into its own corpse. A difficult question which I confine myself here to raise.

But, the objection may be raised: is it not of the essence of philosophical research to aim at establishing a body of coherent and closely linked propositions? By renouncing this ideal do we not reduce this research to being only a formal play, a sterile exercise? Philosophy is nothing if it is not a search; but to search is to hope to find; it is to tend towards something definitive. We must pursue this matter further if we are to avoid misunderstandings.

To be sure, philosophy is essentially a search: it is a search for the Truth. This word, however, displays a fundamental ambiguity which we owe it to ourselves to uncover. In the philosophical sense of this word, Truth is incommensurate with the particular truths which it is given to the man of learning to discover at the end of his patient investigations. It is important to see why this is so.

The property of a particular truth, to whatever order it may belong, is that it is capable of being precisely formulated. Such a truth is even in danger of being confused with the expression in which it is contained, or more exactly of not offering any resistance to this confusion, which is perhaps a corruption. In as much as it is taken by itself, that is to say independently of the inquiry from which it springs, it tends to appear as exterior to the subject. There lies the root of scientism, understood as a degradation of true science. The role of philosophical reflection will be to bring to light the spurious character of every particular truth if it is reduced to an element that can be isolated from knowledge.

A more profound effort could be made to show that, if knowledge is conceived as a mode of possession, it tends to change into the opposite of knowledge. But on the other hand a degradation of this sort is inconceivable when it is a question, not of knowing but of understanding.

It is moreover fitting to observe—and all these remarks go together—that a particular truth is an impersonal truth; its truth value and its impersonal character are inseparable. If I affirm that the conclusion which I have arrived at is true, I mean that every other person in my place proceeding along the right lines, that is in conformity with a certain impersonal logic, would arrive at it just as I did. I am not involved in it; my personality does not count in it. It may be that I have benefited from a privileged intuition on my way to this truth; but this intuition has only opened up for me a discernible path which any one else, it does not matter who, could follow in my footsteps. In the last analysis, the accidental conditions in which I discovered this path are of no consequence; they are likely to interest none but the psychologist or the historian. This is what I shall express by saying that the particular truths depend on *thought in general* (in the Kantian sense).

At first one will be tempted to assert that this is even more true in the case of so-called general truths. But here it behooves us to be careful.

It is quite certain that, if by general truths we mean certain relations which would be disengaged by abstraction from the particular truths to which the different scientific disciplines lead us—that is to say, what we generally call principles, in the Cartesian sense for example—it is certain that these principles also come under thought in general. But what we have got to know is whether these are the kind of principles which philosophy, taken in its essence, undertakes to establish. Really speaking, our problem here is principally one of definition. But philosophy, such as I have always understood it along with many other contemporary thinkers, is oriented to very different ends.

Let me first say briefly that the truth toward which philosophical research aspires is essentially unpossessable; in any event, it cannot be considered or treated as a having.

This is what I meant in the years 1910–1914, when I maintained that metaphysics is above all a philosophy of participation. I was rather struck to observe, at the Philosophical Convention in Paris (in 1937), that Louis Lavelle had made use of this very term, participation, in a sense undoubtedly identical, and consequently quite different from that which it has in Plato. It is the participation of thought in being that we are here concerned with. Once the word participation is brought in we are led to substitute the term being for the term truth. We must, however, avoid all misunderstanding. Formerly I was hasty in affirming what I called the transcendence of being over truth. This is a dangerous and unacceptable way of speaking. Today I would prefer to say that being and truth are identical, but on condition of pointing out, as I did above, the incommensurability of Truth with respect to finite truths to which science gives us access, that is to say, of recognizing explicitly that the methods of verification in reference to which a truth is defined are here inapplicable. With respect to these methods and to these partial truths, the transcendence of being is the transcendence of truth.

Now I would like to examine a little more deeply this affirmation which, taken as a pure abstraction, runs the risk of seeming almost unintelligible.

If, for so vague, so broad an idea of knowledge, we substitute that of *reading,* we understand quite well how, under the objective materiality of a text which is there for everyone, there can lie hidden hierarchies of meaning which are successively revealed to the reader, provided he is endowed with a sufficient power of penetration. This is still saying very little: what intervenes here is a desire for interpretation which is not satisfied with a superficial meaning and aspires to search beyond. The characteristic of a meaning is to reveal itself only to an awareness which is open to receive it; it is in some way a response to an active and persevering expectation, or more precisely, to an exigence. The hierarchy of meanings varies with that of the exigences. But what is true of the reading of a text applies almost exactly to the philosophical search as I understand it. It is in reality an interpretation. Let us keep this word in mind: musical interpretation here offers us an even better term of comparison. Take a musical score; it has signs whose value is rigorously defined for anyone who knows the prevailing system of musical notation. That reading corresponds to what I have called thought in general. But for the musician, whether he performs it or not, it will be a question of interpreting these signs, of discovering the musical meaning of what is at first only a cryptogram. In other words, it will be a matter of proceeding to a true creation to which he is expressly invited or called by the very existence of the score. A re-creation rather than a creation, someone will have me observe. This is both true and false. For the composer who possesses a perfectly distinct awareness of what he has not only willed but understood, it is a question rather of re-creation or even of reproduction. But the one who reads or performs it, being by definition deprived of this preliminary knowledge, can count only on himself, on his own power of sympathetic intuition. It will be necessary for him to surrender himself, to open himself to this mystery of which he has before him only a meager sensible and objective outline. But this creative interpretation toward which he tends is an effective participation in the very inspiration of the composer.

I attach the utmost importance to this comparison, for it permits one to recognize directly that there exists an order situated at once beyond what belongs only to the realm of the valid, but equally beyond what belongs only to the realm of the subjective, understood in the psychological and restrictive sense. It is indeed quite clear that there is a certain reality of Schumann or of Chopin, for example, which the interpreter ought to incarnate, to which he ought to submit himself in an active way, but which does not let itself be rendered by any formula similar to those which translate particular truths. The characteristic of this reality is its power to be misconstrued or betrayed; to be sure, it is of its essence not to impose itself on the mind with the compelling force of a physical text or law. Nevertheless, one would commit the gravest error by attempting to reduce this reality to a simple subjective state, to a passing disposition; this would be to ignore what gives to a work its importance, its value, its virtue.

To acknowledge that an understanding can admit of varying degrees of profundity is implicitly to establish a hierarchy in the apprehension which is ordered to being and not to the valid. And in order to be better understood, I would doubtless have to push further the analysis of the idea of validity: it is inseparable from that of utilization. One should show without difficulty that pragmatism could be introduced only through a systematic confusion between truth and validity. In my opinion it is most desirable for our purpose to bring to light the practical aspect of the notion of validity, to take for example as a reference the validity of a railroad or theatre ticket. The ticket entitles one to such a trip or to such a performance in some determined conditions. A scientific formula is also applicable, although in a different sense, within clearly specified conditions. Validity always implies specification. From this it follows that we tend to represent the formula to ourselves as operating like an automatic click which is produced at the push of a button. I have expressly stated, and I insist on it, that this is nothing but degraded knowledge. But within this realm, such a degradation tends to arise almost inevitably, and only the exercise of reflection, that is to say of the mind as freedom, can effectively counterbalance what must be regarded rather as a process of spiritual sclerosis pure and simple.

Let us concentrate our attention on these words: freedom and reflection. First, freedom. A philosophy worthy of the name cannot but be a philosophy of freedom and that in a double sense.

On the one hand, philosophy is thought centered on Freedom, thought which is given Freedom itself for its content. On the other hand, freedom cannot be conceived except through freedom: it creates or constitutes itself in the act of thinking itself. Here we have a kind of circle which reflection ought to recognize and which has nothing of the vicious in it. The notion of freedom which would demonstrate itself or which could be made to issue forth from a dialectical determinism is a pseudo idea and reflection upon it shows it to be contradictory.

I shall add that, from my point of view, the opposition which some have occasionally sought to establish between the philosophy of being and the philosophy of freedom cannot be maintained. This opposition would be justified only if, while imaginatively "realizing" being, we identified it with substance such as second rate upholders of medieval philosophy or its systematic adversaries have represented it. An authentic philosophy of being is not a philosophy of the thing as Renouvier believed nor is it a philosophy of the static, as Bergson thought. It is evident to me that being, as the great metaphysicians conceived it, transcends the opposition of the static and the dynamic.

The term "reflection" marks more clearly still in what respect my thought is separated from Bergsonian thinking, or at least from the interpretation which is commonly given to it. I think that the philosophical method is reflective *par excellence*. But we are here concerned with a reflection of the second degree which is exercised much less upon immediate consciousness than upon the primary mediations through which the latter is constituted as experience.

Consequently what will be the point of departure of the search which is thus conceived? That will be the consideration of the fundamental situation in which I find myself placed as a human being—let us not yet say as a creature—on the strength of my human condition itself. Here is seen in full light the opposition between a philosophy of the existential type and a philosophy of the Cartesian type—this, even though in Descartes but not in his successors, there may be some points which could be exploited in a non-Cartesian sense. Nevertheless, the *Cogito*, as later in Kant "thought in general," is free of every anthropological mark. According to this impersonal thought the human situation or condition is only an object of consideration as is an other: it [this condition] is treated by this thought as not affecting it; but to this extent this thought is suppressed as situation or as condition. A fictitious suppression; an abstraction by which thought is denied access to being. Here I could not emphasize too strongly my agreement with Heidegger and with Jaspers—particularly with Jaspers who has put so strong an emphasis on limit situations. These latter can only be clarified, but not justified or even explained, if by explanation we mean any sort of deduction from any thing other than these situations themselves.

I think it is necessary to recall here a remark on an uneasiness which is already old and which seems capable of throwing light on the profound meaning of my enterprise.

A metaphysical uneasiness. It seems to me though that a metaphysic is nothing if it is not the act by which an uneasiness is defined and partially— mysteriously—overcome or at least transposed. Uneasiness—but what uneasiness? By that I mean first of all something which is not a curiosity. To be curious is to start out from a certain fixed center, to try to lay hold of, to clutch at, an object of which one had formed only a confused and sketchy representation. I would say that in this sense all curiosity is directed toward the surface. To suffer uneasiness, on the contrary, is not to be sure of one's center; it is to seek one's center, one's equilibrium. This is true of all the meanings of the word uneasiness. If I suffer uneasiness concerning the health of one of my relatives, it means that the doubts or the fears which I entertain concerning it tend to destroy my inner stability. A curiosity tends all the more to become in me an uneasiness as the object on which it bears becomes more a part of me, as it is more closely linked to my moral comfort. (Besides, I will say today that the word "comfort" is inadequate. There is question of a certain order for lack of which I no longer possess myself.) On the other hand an uneasiness is the more metaphysical as it more directly concerns what cannot be separated from me and what cannot be alienated from me in the strong sense of the term without annihilating me. There is a sense in which it is true to say that the only metaphysical problem is: what am I? To this problem all others are reduced, including even the problem of the existence of others. Something powerful and hidden assures me that *if the others do not exist, neither do I*; I cannot attribute to myself an existence which the others would not possess. In this context *I cannot* does not mean *I have not the right*, but rather *that is impossible for me.* If the others elude me, I elude myself, for my substance is made of them.

Can I say that I experience this metaphysical uneasiness as an actually given state? I shall simply say that a circumstance may arise in which I become aware of an uneasiness which on reflection will appear to me as extending infinitely beyond this very circumstance; it displays a quality of permanence, it is not confined to this or that *now*. What is more, as soon as it is formulated, it extends to all the beings whom I can look upon as participating in the same experience as myself. I could not but regard them as experiencing in principle this very uneasiness which is mine.

But the objection could be raised: is not uneasiness traditionally considered as a condition of the antiphilosophical spirit, in contrast to serenity, ataraxia? (The latter will be defined in rather different ways by the diverse philosophical schools.)

I shall reply that if philosophy as a matter of fact tends universally to the establishment of a certain inner peace or harmony, it is no less true that these cannot be given at the start. What is given is the yearning for them and this yearning can only be experienced as a nostalgia, that is to say as an uneasiness. The only question is to ascertain whether one thinks it necessary to put the accent on this initial uneasiness. The more conceptual a philosophy becomes the more it will think it necessary to disregard anything that it might consider as a simple subjective occurrence from which to extract the intelligible content. But to reflection the simple question of emphasis appears to be important; for what is implied here is the value, positive or otherwise, which will be attached to the personal mark. A philosophy of the Hegelian type will push to the limit the idea of an internal dialectic of the concept; it will postulate, or tend to postulate, in principle that the person is, in some accidental way, the simple stage on which this dialectic unfolds in its purity. It will thus make an abstraction of the effect which the person can actually have on a certain life of the empirical subject. At least this will be for that philosophy an ideal, but which a philosophy like the one I am going to outline denies as an ideal.

To be uneasy, I said, is to seek one's center. But these words sufficiently indicate that philosophy, as I see it, is a development which is not pursued only within the subject considered as a spiritual organism, but also within the reality for which this subject is in some way the end—I would even be tempted to say the "stake," for this development seem to me very similar to a game or a drama.

But this is still saying too little. The term "subject" is very ambiguous; that of person would be preferable if unfortunately it had not been so badly abused in recent years. To the extent that this term is opposed to that of the individual it is to be preferred. The most authentic philosophic thought, it seems to me, situates itself at the meeting point of the self and the other. Some hidden power assures me, I repeat, that if the others do not exist neither do I. True, we have here an evidence which has not been universally recognized and which a certain idealism in particular has tended to reject. It remains to be seen what the postulates on which this idealism is founded are worth. "Is it right," I asked not long ago (*Etre et Avoir*, p. 156), "to postu- late in principle the priority of the act by which the I is constituted as a self in relation to the act by which it postulates the reality of the others?" This priority can- not, I think, be affirmed except by virtue of a confusion which Kant has already exposed.

I shall note in passing that no philosophical text has impressed me more strongly than the one in which the American philosopher, W. E. Hocking, in his book *The Meaning of Good in Human Experience*, has es- tablished that we cannot really conceive an apprehend- ing of the other which is not truly an apprehending of ourselves and which confers on our experience its human weight.

When I speak of the meeting point of the self and the other, it is necessary of course to beware of all undue spatialization. We cannot admit for one instant that there exists a sort of demarcation line or seam between the two domains, that of the self and that of the other. Both the history of philosophy as well as the study of literary works, to the extent that they are contributions to the knowledge of man, teach us that the world of the others becomes illumined with an increasingly intense light as the I dispels more of its own darkness and dispels it more heroically.

An influential philosophical tradition, represented in our days for example by Léon Brunschvicg, tends to establish a fundamental distinction between what is proper to each one of us and what is common to all. By so doing it assumes a rational character. I do not claim that this discrimination cannot be made, but I am afraid that it is sterile, that it stems from what I like to call a surface psychology, one that ignores the dimension which belongs to the spiritual life par excellence: depth.

Here again one could find a confirmation of what I said earlier concerning meanings and exigences. The uniqueness in us or in the other can always undoubtedly be labelled an oddity. It can be set aside for disposal in one way or another. But it can also present itself to us as an appeal to a more intimate understanding, to a more personal communication; it can invite us in some mysterious way to a renewal, to a recasting of our categories. On the other hand, the very fact that common or general characteristics permit identification, classification and categorization, makes them only serve to set in motion the most habitual and consequently the least enriching operations of our intelligence. I may observe in passing that this remark, which is surely in keeping with the most profound critical views of a man like Gide, lies at the very basis of all my stage plays.

From this cluster of reflections we can draw the following conclusions. The more we endeavor to communicate with ourselves—by that I mean with what in us at first appears as most recalcitrant to a certain intellectual penetration—the more we free ourselves from the automatism which is nothing but a petrifying of our judgment. On the other hand, to the degree that we surrender ourselves to this automatism, the other ceases to be grasped as other: he is no more than a bundle of abstractions with which we are unable to maintain any living communication. But this non-communication entails on our part a most heavy ransom; it is expressed by an often imperceptible loss of that luminous quality whose presence or absence can be grasped immediately by intuition.

Doubtless someone will confront me with the fact that some very spontaneous persons, incapable of penetrating their own interior darkness—provided such persons exist—are precisely the most apt to communicate with the other. I agree. But this facility for communication among these human beings we are speaking about is imputable to the fact that they are almost entirely exempt from what one so often regards as a superiority: the awareness of self understood in the pejorative sense of the English word "self-conscious." The inability to communicate is linked with self-consciousness, or more precisely with the fact that the self remains withdrawn and shrivelled up inside. One could therefore, it appears, distinguish two levels on which communication becomes real: the one is that of naiveté or of what one could call the mind of a child, which precedes the consciousness of the self; the other level, infinitely more elevated, is that in which the self has in some way triumphed over itself.

By definition the philosopher has behind him a lost paradise. (This state of pure spontaneity is that of the child who reaches without effort the shores of the other.) He cannot dream of going back to the hither side of self-consciousness; it is therefore only by an effort of transcendence that he can hope to re-establish ways of communication that are somehow sealed. It is even necessary that he undertakes this exploration with the desire, nay more, with the fixed intention of emerging into a world of concrete thought in which he will find himself on a level with his neighbor, in which he will see in a purified light what the pale light of daily relations scarcely permits him to have an inkling of.

According to me it is precisely there that philosophic involvement, of which explicit mention has not yet been made, is situated. In contrast to a certain desire for seclusion, from which a particular contemporary thinker is perhaps not always exempt and which is especially discernible among many poets, I shall say that the philosopher, as I conceive him, ought to push to its limit the desire for communication. But this can be effectively accomplished only in a roundabout way. Philosophically, the road which leads from me to the other passes through my own depths. This does not, however, mean that these depths are accessible to introspection left to its resources alone. It is even permissible to think that in this realm the part which belongs to introspection is relatively small. Much more considerable is the part of experience, in the broad sense, that is to say of the experience of the self in contact with life, an experience which can affect the most diverse, sometimes the most disconcerting, modalities. In what concerns me personally, I am bound to recognize, as I said at the beginning, that this experience has most often taken the form of dramatic creation; it is as though my characters had been the essential reagents conjured up by some sort of supra-conscious imagination for permitting my most intimate thought to proceed to a crystallization of which it would not have been capable on its own, by that I mean when left only to the resources of the ego. In this way the link which I established at the beginning between my dramatic writings and my philosophical work in the strict sense is rendered more precise.

Metaphysical Journal
(1938-1943)

Paris, January, 1938

Here I would like to ask myself what we spontaneously mean by a profound idea or feeling.

At first blush are we not tempted to say that a profound idea is qualified by its content? A profound idea would bear on a hidden reality, not on a simple appearance. But this interpretation does not take us very far. This is because reflection shows that the distinction between appearance and reality does not obviously bear on objects or on objectively differentiated realms. One may wonder if what we call reality is not another way of looking at what under certain conditions presents itself as a simple appearance.

I shall place myself on a phenomenological standpoint and ask what happens when an idea or thought presents itself to me as profound; in other words, when it is marked by a certain quality which is lacking in the prevailing customary ideas, in those that constitute my everyday equipment. It is important to observe that the profound idea is not given to me essentially as the unaccustomed, at least if unaccustomed means odd. To be more precise, we should say that strangeness does not suffice to characterize a profound idea as such.

There is in fact a strangeness in the spiritual order which may be compared to that of an ephemeral arrangement or gathering, of clouds for example. This strangeness does not occur without the awareness of an accidental and therefore precarious grouping of different elements. There are some thoughts that are of this nature. I am thinking of paradoxes such as one comes across every now and then in people like Oscar Wilde. It is, however, necessary to observe that strangeness in this case can be deceptive. In what way? Obviously under the guise of an effect of perspective: to the degree that this strange thought, which looms up like an undulation in the ground, breaks the drabness around us, it is given to us as leading perhaps somewhere, like a possible road to some other place. In this matter, experience will serve as always only as a test. Instead of preserving with respect to this thought the onlooking attitude of the amateur, my concern will be to use it positively as a springboard, as a point of departure, in order to ascertain whether it possesses a propulsive power or not. I will also be able to ask myself whether it unfolds or develops when I come near to it, or whether, on the contrary, it retains the deceiving, the indigent immutability of a stage setting.

Already we can see that an idea manifests itself to us as profound in so far as it appears to empty itself into a beyond. Strictly speaking this beyond cannot by definition be given; neither is it any more inferred but only fore-shadowed or anticipated provided that this anticipation be in the form of a premonition rather than as the result of a logical argument. The most precise metaphor that occurs to my mind is that of a channel which would present itself to us from an angle, stretching toward an opening which as yet is only conjectured. Thus it is that certain landscapes have aroused in me a genuinely spiritual emotion. I dream of the approaches to Ragusa when one arrives by sea from Corçula.

I would therefore be inclined to ask myself whether the experience of the profound in its essence would not be linked to the feeling of a promise implicit in the intuitive glimpse of what lies ahead.

But it is necessary to push the analysis still further. It is not enough to say that the thought which is given to us as profound is the one which appears to open out into the distance; it is also necessary to ask what this distance is. At this point we are obliged to go beyond the limits of a purely spatial representation. We do not experience this distance as an elsewhere or another place; I should rather say that it is something "very near." Here we would do well to express ourselves in precise terms. At bottom the very distinction between the here and the elsewhere is transcended. To be more precise, it is in this case reversed. How can that be? This distance presents itself to us in the interior of a certain domain which I am tempted to say is *nostalgically ours*. Actually I think we should have recourse to the myth of exile in order to weigh this situation which, from the perspective of an exclusively spatial logic, seems contradictory. We ought therefore to focus our attention on the condition of a being who has the awareness of not coinciding with his *here*, or who experiences his place as contingent—in opposition to a certain center which should be his real place, but which, in the actual conditions to which he is subjected, can only be thought of as a yonder, as the center of his nostalgia.

Here we might profitably recall certain childhood experiences which are made up of affective imagination and which gravitate around secret hiding places, mysterious gardens, etc. Such experiences I have described in metaphysical language as an absolute *here* which at the same time would be an *out there*. Naturally it is possible that experiences of this kind may on the other hand be amenable to a psychoanalytic interpretation. However, leaving aside that this interpretation is probably not necessary, I seriously doubt that it may be able to help us to elucidate the feeling of depth.

Perhaps the objection may be raised that in this entire discussion we remain on the spatial, that is to say on the metaphorical, plane and that we do not clarify the feeling of depth unless we succeed in despatializing it altogether. But I may observe that we have already realized here a partial despatialization to the degree that we have reversed the normal relation between the here and the elsewhere. We could say that an absolute here, while not coinciding with my contingent here, exists in space only as not being in it. [Moreover I seriously doubt that we can pursue to the limit every process of despatialization. We would probably have to give up the opposition formerly established by Bergson. I am personally convinced that, in introducing and elaborating the notion of lived space, Eugène Minkowski has on this point made an important advance in relation to the original Bergsonian thought. It is true that in Bergson himself we would undoubtedly find some indications which are oriented in this direction; but to me he does not seem to have exploited them sufficiently.][1]

It would be interesting to find out to what extent, within the temporal register itself, an analogous paradox seems to be linked to the understanding of depth. The profound idea reaches far; it points to a going forward that can be done only within time. It is like an

[1] The phrases placed within brackets were written in 1945 and render the function of complementing or clarifying.

intuitive plunge into what can be attained only by means of a search which develops within duration. Nevertheless we would not account for the nuance which I have here in mind if we put the emphasis exclusively on the fact that a profound thought is like an investment for the future. Or rather the future which is here anticipated is not at any rate evoked as pure novelty in relation to what is actually given. The future seems to be most mysteriously in harmony with the most distant past; I was going to say, to the *deepest* past. Actually between the past and the profound there exists a certain affinity. We might truthfully say, however obscure such a notion may appear, that in the bosom of depth the past and the future are joined together. This dimension is to what I call the present what the absolute Here is to the contingent here. This zone in which the *now* and the *then* tend to merge, as did the *near* and the *far* a while ago, is without doubt what we call eternity. From this point of view, we would be tempted to say that the Nietzschean idea of the eternal return not only makes sense but also gives us in some way the very range of the profound. This is so in spite of the possibility that such an idea might turn out to be mythical or rationally unjustifiable when we consider it in itself, and especially when we stop at the pseudo-scientific arguments on which it claims to be based.

Now we would do well to ask ourselves whether these remarks are supported or can be completed by an analysis of a deep feeling.

One will readily admit that the depth of a feeling is judged by the resistance it can offer to the conditions which would logically seem necessary to bring about its dissolution. (For example, separation in the case of love; or for the believer the fact of living in a milieu in which no one shares his faith, etc.) But this does not enlighten us, except quite indirectly and by ever so little, on what is appropriately meant by depth.

Let us observe, first of all, that as a feeling grows in depth, it does not expressly reveal itself as such to immediate consciousness but only to the reflection which is exercised on it subsequently. Moreover, such a reflection bears on the self in so far as it is other. As a rule, when I experience a deep feeling, precisely because I yield to it or surrender myself to it, I do not consider it as profound; I do not value it; I do not appreciate it. It may happen, however, that I have to examine myself here and now concerning the depth of a feeling which I experience (if only because of having to make a decision which would be justifiable in my own eyes only if I had the assurance that it was dictated by a deep feeling). Reflection is here linked to a power of anticipation which bears on my future in so far as it is mine: it is possible only if I cut myself loose in some way from my present. But this enables us to discern right away the temporal reference which is attached to depth. The latter would seem comparable to the *"surface"* [the financial standing] of a debtor, that is to say, to the credit which one can reasonably make available to him. Nevertheless, the problem is not thereby resolved. At most we are in a position to indicate the data. What is the criterion which enables us to appreciate this credit, supposing that this word "criterion" is suitable, which I doubt? Can this criterion be clearly pointed out and thus designated? Can it be directly recognized? It is almost certain that this is not the case. But then must we not desist from speaking of a criterion? Are we dealing, not with the determination of the feeling itself, but with a relation, let us say more precisely with a secret affinity, between the feeling and the self? But in expressing ourselves thus, are we not running the risk of indulging in abstractions? For a feeling is genuinely deep to the degree that it does not allow itself to be really dissociated from the self and that the self discovers a oneness with it. This need not be equivalent to the awareness of a harmony or especially of ease: it is possible that the self be discovered only in despair or in tragedy.

Thus we would be led to catch a glimpse of the fact that a deep feeling is one in which the essence itself is engaged. However, this statement is still vague, or even ambiguous.

In general we shall be inclined to admit that if a deep feeling can suddenly come to birth, its emergence should at least have been prepared underground. But this is fundamentally an *a priori* view. Besides it is instructive as regards the exigence which such an affirmation supposes. It is our basic postulate that if a feeling is deep, it must spring from roots within a distant past, even though we make allowance for a "metabolism" by means of which this deep-rooted feeling has been able to reveal itself successively under very different aspects. The deep feeling is here interpreted in terms of primitive tendencies, which in themselves can be sufficiently indeterminate. Every naturalistic interpretation of depth, I think, will be oriented in this direction. It will tend to treat depth as not being in reality a value, unless by a decree that is seemingly quite arbitrary one declares on the contrary that the primordial as such reveals an intrinsic value in opposition to all the adventitious elements, to all the subsequent determinations which come to superimpose themselves on it in the course of its evolution. Thus is defined what one might call the pseudo-mystique of the *Ursprünglichkeit*, of the primordial as such. But such an interpretation does not seem able to stand up to reflection for one second. There is actually no reason why the essential should be given at the beginning or outset. It may well be that in its origin the essential is strictly speaking indiscernible. The original determinations may be the least essential of all. On the other hand though, it may be necessary to consider them as manifesting at the very least a seminal value. [If the seminal is not identified with the profound, perhaps that is because it has its future before it and because in this sense it belongs to the order of chance or simply of possibility. But a possibility as such cannot by judged as being either profound or superficial. The profound is situated on another level. By that I do not mean that it exists. It would rather be on the other side of existence, while the possible lies on this side. But if the profound is on the other side of existence, then perhaps it cannot be *evoked* without inflicting on the existent a certain unreality. With respect to the profound, what merely exists hardly exists.]

One might ask whether these remarks which are all directed beyond what any description can represent do not point to a metaphysics of essence. It is possible that it may well be so; but it is evident that the hidden essence which here throws out its intermittent rays does in no way resemble the essence which is affirmed by traditional philosophies. We cannot reach it by an act of abstraction. Moreover, this last verb "reach" is in this context altogether inadequate. I shall say, not without hesitation, that the essence is such that it can much sooner shed light than let light be shed upon it; much less can it be described. The hidden essence is central; make no mistake about that. To the degree that it is present to consciousness, the latter can itself be treated as a luminous source. Moreover, it is evident that

within this perspective one would be inclined to reconcile and ultimately to identify essence and value, but
this should be done only on condition of deliberately
rejecting, once and for all, the act by which one would
pretend to convert them into intelligible objects, into
noeta. Every claim of this kind virtually denies and
destroys what it claims to affirm.

But from this point of view, it is perhaps possible to
shed light on the paradox which consists in affirming
the identity of the near and the far in the bosom of the
profound. The essence is near, since from it there emanates the clarity without which nothing would exist for
me; it is infinitely distant in that I cannot move toward
it, that is, I cannot endeavor to approach it without it
promptly disappearing. Here the myth of Eurydice becomes revelatory.

[1939]

Paris, April 24, 1939

        This morning I clearly saw the fundamental ambiguity of what I call *my life*, depending on whether I treat it as a succession of moments or events, or as something which is capable of being given, sacrificed, or lost. Perhaps it is only in this second sense that one can attach any significance to the idea of immortality.

In the first sense, my life appears as being limited, as occupying an interval between two dates, as furnishing the material for a chronology. At times it can become sufficiently external to me for me to look upon it in this light, to sadden, for example, at the thought that these events have been few in number. I shall come to consider them then as little islands separated by empty spaces. I shall envisage my future from the same point of view; the events that I have yet to live are doubtless less numerous than those which I have already lived. In as much as I thus withdraw from my life in order to observe it, I shall say that it is becoming a corpse. From this life, it is precisely life that is ebbing away.

If now I resume my life like a man resumes his domicile I find myself engaged *in* and oriented *toward*. Engaged in what? Oriented toward what? It is not easy to reply to these questions except to the extent that I engage in some kind of creative work, for which I feel somewhat indispensable. This creative work, of course, can present some diverse aspects.

But it is necessary to observe that ultimately this creative work can degrade itself in two ways:

(1) in tasks accomplished from day to day more or less automatically;

(2) in interest taken in events which unroll like a serialized novel: the world is apprehended like a movie picture.

Here and there one is separated from despair only by a thin partition, since one experiences one's own life as useless, as unreal, or as absent. Despair, however, can appear as a means of recuperation on condition that it becomes a matter for reflection. To recognize this absence is in some way to transmute it into presence.

But to resume my life effectively is to experience it anew as fullness: negatively this means that I cease to liken it to a succession of more or less trifling episodes. If now I recall one or other of these episodes, it will take on a value, a depth, in proportion to this newly discovered plenitude. This again means that I desist from comparing my life with such another, more blessed and more fulfilled. Plenitude is beyond comparison.

But at the same time is it not evident that plenitude is here linked to consecration? No life is creative except to the degree that it is consecrated. On the other hand, it is from this very consecration that the gift of my life becomes possible, since this gift (which from a different point of view can seem contradictory and even foolish) realizes only one more step on the road of consecration. To refuse to give my life in some extreme circumstances would be, not to preserve it, but to mutilate it. It is as though sacrifice were its very fulfilment, as though to lose it were the means of saving it.

However, we must here foresee the counter-attack of a purely critical reflection: one may well imagine that the feeling of plenitude reaches its peak in the act by which man is wholly engaged in behalf of what he serves. But can we say, without playing on words, that thereby he actually saves what he appears to lose? Is not this feeling of being full or uplifted an entirely subjective datum which, together with the subject, is swallowed up in death?

It would indeed be necessary to submit to a rigorous reflection that affirmation: "I sacrifice my life in order that. . . ." The expression is definitely inadequate. It tends to establish, or seems to presuppose, an almost unintelligible relation between me and my life, since the latter seems to be identified with a having, which I would renounce. Here we have a mode of representation that is secondary or accidental and distorting. In this act, my life is really the subject; it consecrates itself by sacrificing itself. It is moreover necessary to observe—and this is crucial—that, to the degree that this act is reflected upon, it tends to change its nature. It is extremely rare that absolute sacrifice takes cognizance of itself. More precisely, in taking cognizance of itself, it is in danger of succumbing to a literary form of expression which alters it.

Here, as elsewhere, genuinely philosophical reflection is obliged to rediscover the act itself beneath the growth which threatens to cover it.

Again, we can say that, when I sacrifice my life, it is not *something* I abandon in order to obtain something else. If I may say so, it is the exact opposite of something, of this or that thing. It is the whole or it presents itself as being the whole. Here however a discrepancy seems to arise. It is really necessary that there should be something outside of this whole, something that ought to be safeguarded at all cost; otherwise the sacrifice would be without an object. This "other thing" is posited by me as absolutely real. Its reality is even measured by the fullness of the sacrifice which I accept in order that it may be saved. This sacrifice therefore becomes the testimony which I offer to this reality which is treated as independent of me; it is my way of attesting it. Death takes on here a meaning, or its meaning, both in so far as it is thought as absolute and in so far as it is denied to the advantage of a reality which it is incapable of reducing. At the root of absolute sacrifice, we find so to say not only an "I die," but a "you: you shall not die." Or again, "because I die, you shall be saved," or more strictly, "my death increases your chances of living." Actually it seems that sacrifice takes on its meaning only in relation to a reality that is susceptible of being threatened, that is, a reality historically given and consequently exposed to the forces of destruction which are brought to bear on whatever endures.

Here again the subjectivist objection will demand a close scrutiny. One might indeed say that the sacrifice attests only the value which the subject attaches to anything that in itself is perhaps not a reality at all. Patriotism does not prove the reality of the fatherland.

Here we have a crop of difficulties, for it is beyond doubt that the heroic act tends to create or even to confirm in being the very thing it latches on to (compare the martyrs in the history of the Church).

Paris, April 25, 1939

What stands in our way is a rigid and over-simplified notion of objective reality, conceived as existing simply for recognition and as having no need of us whatsoever.

It is most interesting to note that, from a certain point of view, absolute sacrifice cannot but appear as a deception. How can I help remarking that the reality to which I refer is such only in relation to a source of evaluations which coincides with my life and is extinguished when the latter perishes? Consequently, the illusion which lies at the basis of sacrifice would consist in forgetting this dependence and in treating as existing by itself what in reality exists only in relation to me. My life is here pictured as a magic lantern which projects its light on figures that by themselves are devoid of relief and color. But if I conceive myself as being the creator of some spectacle, it is definitely absurd to suppress my reality in order that the spectacle may continue.

Sacrifice can therefore be accomplished only to the degree that consciousness ceases to treat itself as the center of projection.

The problem which I would like to tackle would consist in asking whether a phenomenological representation of death as absolute is compatible with a meta-phenomenological position of immortality. A position which would evidently involve the affirmation of Grace, that is to say, of the self as called, redeemed, elevated. What renders the position so difficult is the fact that the absolute gravity of death, as I have said, appears as the supreme guarantee of reality for the Cause to which the I is immolated. In order that this absolute gravity be safeguarded, I must at least admit to ignoring absolutely what in me is capable of surviving this radical test. It even seems possible that what I prefer in me, that on which my heart is set, is destined to perish irretrievably. To say that, phenomenologically, death should be treated as an absolute is to deny the possibil-

ity of my looking beyond, of anticipating something
which would be without tomorrow—an exit from a
tunnel. This boils down to the fact that my death
cannot be considered by me as being an event. It is an
event only for others, in as much as it *his* death, not
mine, and, if I believe I can anticipate it, it is in so far
as I coincide imaginatively with an other for whom it
will be "*his* death."

Paris, April 26, 1939

Sacrifice as the measure which measures, that is to
say, as conferring its grandeur on the reality which it
measures.

My life as phenomenological absolute, but as maintaining with myself an essentially ambiguous relation.
For I do not possess it except from the moment it
ceases to possess me. I can be left to the mercy of my
life in nostalgia, regret or covetousness.

On the other hand, we must examine how every trial,
even one which in appearance is merely endured, like
sickness, can be transmuted into sacrifice, that is to say,
offered up. But we must probe into this more deeply
and not be satisfied with a sort of edifying and ready-
made language.

We will equally have to disengage the sort of dialectic which is carried on at the very core of the notion of
the absolute. The word "notion" is however inadequate
in this context. It is the essence of my life that I can
appear to myself as absolute: the basis of a radical
egoism, of a lived solipsism. The experience which others have is then for me as non-existent. Or its existence
is like a phantom in contrast to the substantial reality
of my pleasure or of my distress.

Paris, April 30, 1939

While reading over my notes of April 24th last, I feel
the need of pointing out the ambiguity of the word *life*.
If I withdraw from my life in order to reflect on it, I
cannot help seeing it as a current which is destined to
be swallowed up in death. From this point of view, it
seems that everything is already lost. This is the dizzi-
ness to which I alluded in my address to the Interna-
tional Congress of Philosophy in 1937. I find myself in
the presence of something which lets itself go exactly
like a body dragged down by its weight or like a feather
blown by the wind. In contrast to this, all work, whatever it be, all effort is oriented in an opposite direction.
It is an uphill climb in the course of which we could let
outselves go, that is, be carried away. We are here in a
realm of thoughts which are peculiarly Bergsonian. It is
impossible not to see that it is only in this direction
that the mysterious notion of immortality can be significant.

[1940]

Lyons, December 10, 1940

If I am not mistaken, these are the first philosophical notes which I am jotting down since the disaster.[1] In my thought, these should have formed the preliminary steps of a study, long since in progress, on time and eternity. Once more I would like to devote myself to the inquiry concerning the relations between me and my past.

But first, what is my past? It occurs to me today that it is not truly a "given." The unity which I attribute to "my past," when I pronounce these two words, belongs to it only in thought. What is given to me is either some shreds (I am not sure whether this metaphor is entirely acceptable), or a certain quality, a certain indefinable sign; and even that would have to be examined closely to see what it is.

Actually, when I say "my past," without realizing it,

[1] With good reason, some would be astonished not to find in the pages which follow any mention of the events which befell our country since 1939. To such persons I would like to say that, for the last five years, I have kept another far more detailed diary, in which I deal exclusively with these events lived from day to day. But I doubt if this diary deserves to be put into the hands of the public.

I assume. . . . What exactly do I assume? My assumption seems only to crystallize into a certain image—which, however, can "fade" to an extreme degree—for example, that of a complete collection of memories or lived experiences. Let us leave aside for the moment the thorny question whether some memories or lived experiences can really form a collection. At any rate, when I say "my past," I imply that everything that has happened to me constitutes a whole which is capable of being augmented so long as I live. Some things have happened to me; some others will. But I am convinced that, without actually accounting for it, I make reference to some possible history of my existence. Whatever forms a part of my past would have to be placed within this history, taken authentically and exhaustively. Consequently, it is permissible to ask if a rigorous reflection upon my past would not necessarily imply a preliminary examination of what is a history or a narrative, and of the conditions in which a history or narrative can be construed. Perhaps after all it would be necessary to introduce the notion of a chronicle, understood as a sort of array of events which succeed one another within time. Such a thing happened to me, then such another. Here we might recall to mind a diary like that of Pepys in which everything is scrupulously noted, and equably recorded. I am absolutely sure that each human existence, my existence—and that whoever I may be—can be the occasion for a similar diary. The words *compact, dense,* express sufficiently well the impression which similar notations give. But I must add that the repetition of incidents of organic or organico-psychical life has something heart-breaking about it. *It is a fullness which is nothing but emptiness.*

(I insist on pointing out that I am deliberately ad-

dressing myself here to a valid critique of the Bergsonian notion of a wholly present past. This is a notion
which I think is decidedly inacceptable.)

We are there in an order which implies constant
replacement. Normally, the meal which I have just
taken or am going to take ought in my consciousness to
replace the one which I took yesterday, or eight days
ago, or better still eighteen years ago. (This would not
apply to the exceptional case in which one of these
meals had taken on for me a "historic" character, because it had been extraordinarily good, or because it
had made me sick, or because I had taken it in the
company of such a person.) I shall therefore say that
the chronicle has a certain unnatural quality: it brings
about in so far as is possible the juxtaposition of what
should not have been juxtaposed at all. I should not
have been able to keep in view, that is within the field
of consciousness, the succession of meals or of visceral
incidents, etc., all at once. All that has meaning only on
condition of being lived progressively as it happens, and
cannot be displayed without being distorted. Now the
characteristic of a chronicle is to be in some manner a
display.

In brief, this amounts to saying that it is essential to
life not to let itself be displayed (the image I have in
mind is that of a piece of *folded* cloth or paper). In this
way, the selection which imposes itself on the narrator
or historian would be justified. In short, this would be
the occasion for reflecting on tedium. It is by means of
the folding that life escapes tedium, but naturally this
spatial image of a folding is in a sense altogether inadequate. It would be necessary to ask how it imposes itself
on the mind: it is linked to a certain effect of perspective. The enfolding is linked to the periodicity of which
we are always inclined to make too much abstraction.

Lyons, December 11, 1940

I would like to resume the thread of my reflections from yesterday. This thread is in danger of being lost or entangled.

I meant that my past in its completeness can only be envisaged in terms of an allegedly exhaustive account. But I can only imagine this account as drawn up and, up to a certain point, as converting the succession into a simultaneity. But the kind of succession that is realized within an existence cannot be *made simultaneous* without losing its character and its meaning.

We could express the same thing by saying that life comprises an enormous part given to what is consumed or used up. There we have an element to which no survival whatever could be granted, not even the wholly ideal one which the narrator guarantees to the thing narrated.

(Thus one would tend absolutely to reject the idea, as it were, of a diluted immortality which would belong in principle to whatever has been lived: immortality can only be conceived as concentrated on nuclei or centers endowed with stability and resistance in contrast to that flux, to that alternation of absorption and reabsorption.)

All that militates against the idea of the past as a reservoir from which each person would draw—an idea peculiarly hard to efface. In order to exorcise it, however, it would perhaps suffice to understand that there is no reservoir unless a difference exists between a container and a corresponding content, and that this distinction does not make any sense in this case.

Nevertheless, returning to the objection, someone may say: "Am I not obliged to think of the existence of some sum total of what has happened to me, of what has been lived by me?"

I think we must combat this very notion of a sum total. No sum total is possible except of elements that have been retained or preserved so as to be capable of being added up. But my reflections of yesterday tend to show precisely that nothing of the kind is here conceivable. What has been consumed or used up or dissipated is diametrically opposed to what has been retained.

This would amount to saying that there is in life, in my life, an essential aspect whereby it cannot be *totalized*; and perhaps this pure dissipation is one of the conditions of the real building-up of a being. Dissipation which in the last analysis bears on the insignificant. We cannot deny the insignificant except in the name of abstract and arbitrary principles, and by rejecting a positive given of our experience. There is surely an effective liberation in recognizing that this insignificant exists as such. Perhaps it would be preferable not to make use of the verb "to exist," since it is actually of the essence of this insignificant to vanish, to go up in smoke. But at the same time, because we are capable of attention, we have the extraordinary power to arrest the insignificant, to intercept it, to give it a stability, a value, and thereby even to change it.

However, and in spite of this last remark, how can one not see that by recognizing the insignificant as such, we run the risk of treating our own selves, in the last resort, as smoke, as pure consumption? In this there is a temptation. Can we make allowance for this Heraclitianism? There is the question. In other words, from the fact that my past is not a whole, must I infer that it is nothing? That would be, I think, an absurd conclusion. When I say "my past," I intend "something," and what my reflection has shown me is simply that there is a faulty way of interpreting or representing this something.

What then do I have in view when I speak of my past? It is very difficult to put the question in precise terms. Actually if I reply, which seems reasonable, that it is always a question of a certain perspective, governed by my "lived" present, I shall be irresistibly drawn to imagine that this perspective is relative to an "in itself" comparable to an object, to a solid which it is never given to me to see except from a certain angle. Now, in conceiving this "in itself," do I not re-establish the notion of my past as totality? To be honest, I am not altogether sure. It is evident that the cathedral of Chartres, for example, cannot in any way be considered as the sum total of the views that I can get of it, or of the aspects which it presents, or again of some details which can be noted in it. It transcends all that without it being easy to see, however, what this transcendence must positively mean.

But let us examine the difference closely; it can be instructive. For me who contemplate the cathedral of Chartres it is a being, or, if one wishes, a world which can be envisaged as the expression of the materialization of a thought *only within certain relations.*

Even I can be considered from the outside, for example by the one who studies my work or intends to write my biography. Nay more, I can to a degree make my critic's or my biographer's point of view my own. But when I speak of my past, it is precisely at this point of view that I *do not place myself.* Or rather is it that I do not adopt a sort of intermediary and untenable position between living my past and contemplating it? It is this that we are going to have to probe into. I am somewhat fatigued this evening and I am afraid of messing up this idea by pursuing it further.

Yes, it really seems that when I speak of my past I turn into a memorialist without, however, severing the vital links which bind me to what I recall.

It would be necessary to apply this to the problem of knowing what takes place when I try to recall and to describe the person I was at such a determinate period of time. Is it not a *personage* which I claim to revive? What am I in relation to this personage? Is there a means of turning to account my preceding remarks? This is what I do not see clearly yet.

Lyons, December 12, 1940

I can only reconstitute this personage that I was, when I was married for example, from certain elements. It is surely not given to me as a unity within memory. On the other hand, this "I" that I was then was not a personage; it *became* a personage subsequently in as much as it detached itself, or in as much as it became possible for me to treat it as though it were detached. Besides, one should not doubt that there exists here an optical illusion. This detachment cannot be absolute; it is by a veritable artifice that I am in a position to regard as a *characterizable* personage the one I was then.

I have the impression that these remarks terminate in an impasse. I do not see how they could lead to anything new or instructive, at least for the moment.

The observation I recorded yesterday evening is more interesting. To recall my past in its totality is to adopt a hybrid attitude, that is, to contemplate the lived without being resolved to cease living it. One might say that this attitude, even though it be contradictory, is relative to a movement by which I tend in some way to withdraw from my life. It is this withdrawal that we should attempt to grasp.

At the same time it is clear that these words "to withdraw from one's own life" have a meaning and that it is very difficult to define this meaning. One would have to be able to see what it means to be in his life or outside it. Is not that just a bad metaphor?

Montana, December 21, 1940

I re-read those notes; they seem to constitute an interesting beginning. But we must sort the questions which suggested themselves with those first reflections. One of the most important will consist in asking what to retain signifies in contrast to, to dissipate, to permit to be lost, etc. . . . We should not be taken in by current terms in psychology, such as subconscious or unconscious awareness, let alone fall prey to mythology.

When I think of certain scenes of my early childhood, for example a certain winding street called Général-Foy, one late afternoon (I could not have been more than three), I am inclined to think that there has occured on the one hand an initial survival—accidental or otherwise: one would first have to ask what "accidental" here means—and then, on the other hand, subsequently, a stereotyping. In the second case, the word "to retain" has the meaning of "to fix." If the same word is applicable to the first case does it have the same meaning? Probably not. At first blush, this seems to me important.

Can we admit as a hypothesis, and without going deeply into it, that certain experiences have the power to survive themselves, or more precisely, to re-impose themselves on consciousness and that the latter, in response to this recurrence, proceeds to a fixation which is a schematization? (*Das fixierte Erlebnis wird leblos:* The fixated experience becomes lifeless.) Still we would have to render this notion of survival intelligible, or perhaps enquire to what extent it ought to be (if for example our demand for intelligibility does not imply here an arbitrary transposition into one domain of what has meaning only in another domain). We could for example imagine that each experience, each *Erlebnis* is *moored* in varying degree to what we rather inappropriately call the instant in which this experience arises, in its spatio-temporal place, its here and now. What earlier I termed survival would actually be only the floating, free quality of the experience in question.

We must examine this possibility. Does it really make sense? Can we consider this mooring as being able to comprise degrees?

Ultimately, the perfectly moored (I provisionally grant that this word has a meaning) experience is the one which could not at all outlive itself.

Reflection here unveils a paradox. I cannot speak of a mooring except in terms of an element that is unvarying or treated as such. But what is it that, in the matter which occupies us, could play the role of an invariant?

(In other words, could we ask: what will the words "here and now" cover? Can they imply any attachment or absence of attachment to a place?)

If on reflection this question is found not to admit of any solution at all, it seems that we must reject this mode of interpretation.[1] The paradox consists in this that an experience, incapable of surviving itself or of reviving in a new context, seems powerless to be conceived precisely as attached to a fixed element.

---

[1] I note in passing that my method seems to consist in the alternation of a kind of "prospection" and reflection. This method analyses and criticizes what has been given by means of this initial "prospection."

Here again, reflection would be called for on the very notion of fixity (and indirectly on the possible usage outside the material world of a metaphor borrowed from the domain of pure materiality).

At this moment I wonder if this does not connect with the reflections to which I recently devoted myself on the subject of *happening to*. It seems that of certain things (this vague expression is hardly avoidable) I may not be able to say literally that they happened to me. They are such as do not outlive themselves, or which I could not in any way relate. (To me death appears to be something—I would not necessarily say an event—of this order which I can succeed in defining only negatively.) [2]

I perceive a very clear link between this group of remarks and my reflections in Lyons. My past can be treated as a collectivity only to the extent that it is treated as a group of stereotyped, fixed, categorized elements. My trip to Yugoslavia, to the degree that I relate it, were it only to myself, is thus reduced to a certain sum of elements that can be counted. But at the same time I reckon that my past is not exhausted by this sum. If I reflect upon these elements, they manifest themselves to me as partial, fragmentary crystallizations, I might even say coagulations, of something fluid which surrounds and permeates them. But this fluid element tends to evaporate, or at least to become imperceptible, when I relate this trip, and especially to the degree that I repeat this account. (Cf. the words of Henri in *The Broken World.*[3]) Correlatively, let us

[2] We are of course dealing here with *my* death, not that of some other person whose death is inevitably an event for me. (Notes of 1958)

[3] "I will say to you that I have narrated this account eleven times already. It has exhausted my memories completely; I know it by heart, but I have forgotten everything that I saw."

note that these elements are more and more depersonalized; my account could be given by a third party
taking my place. The account in the first person becomes an account in the third person: "Gabriel sailed
to Sussex on such a day and on such a boat. He first put
in at Rab, etc. . . ." For me, to the extent that I relate
my own past in this manner, it is depersonalized (like a
path originally traced by me but which would become a
path for everyone, a path which everyone can take). By
the same token, I become a stranger to myself in social-
izing my past, in rendering it common;[4] I withdraw
from it. But it could take just a chance, a breath, for me
to revive this past as mine across the account which
adulterated it, as though I embraced it anew, the very
thing which I had disowned in retailing it as a piece of
news.

If I go back to the example chosen of a trip to
Yugoslavia, I must add that the fluid element in which
the recounted memories are steeped is intimately
marked by the fact that this experience was *ours*, my
wife's and mine. We should probe deeper into this. But
immediately I pass beyond this particular case in order
to ascertain whether this awareness of "our" is not present even when I was, objectively speaking, alone. That
would be true to the degree that I have essentially and
for always become for myself a "thou," that I form a
community which is never allowed to be reduced to a
superficial subjectivity.

Only through this presence of a "thou" in me do I
seem able to account for this intimate, mysterious quality which affects for me my past. (It is surely necessary
to add that a coalescence tends to be formed between

[4] Common. The original reads "banal (au sens de four banal)."
There is an allusion here to banal in its feudal sense: the banal
oven used by all. (Ed.)

this almost unattainable, unobjectifiable "thou" and all those who were "thou" for me, that is, "dear ones"—a pity that the French language does not lend itself so easily to the expression of these essential truths!—I am obliged to say *the beloved.*

From there we must go back to the question I raised earlier this afternoon on the subject of a fixed element. To this element, it seems, there ought to have been indissolubly moored the non-floating data of my experience, those which cannot enter into a collectivity.

Again I make a note of this point: I have spoken earlier of survival. But would it not lead to an extraordinary reversal perspective? From the moment in which there is fixation, there is not and there cannot be survival, but instead "mortification," in the sense in which one speaks of a dead skin. It is actually here that the word "preserved" finds its application as when we speak of "preserved" (canned) fruit. To the extent that by memory we understand a certain life, a certain real living on, it would be necessary to say paradoxically that my memories are made up only of things which I do not remember. Here we are moving toward Proust. This real survival would be capable of being grasped only in a flashing sort of way, in a vanishing way also inasmuch as it precedes all stereotyping.

Montana, December 23, 1940

I am extremely dissatisfied with what I wrote the day before yesterday. Nothing is definitely settled. What I wrote about the "thou" in the "I" is unintelligible. I must succeed in clarifying what I saw in a vague sort of way.

I think that this is the abstract expression of an experiment I have tried since I was a child, that of dialoging with myself. This dialog had probably nothing in common with the subject-object relation of the philosophers. On the contrary, it refers directly with those relations that I mentioned in *Belonging and Availability*. Could we exploit the idea of a communal self, that is, of a community between uncountable "elements" (an unsuitable word), from which the data of experience would distribute themselves, these data being consequently capable of being personalized in greatly varying degrees?

One might ask how I can speak of a community in which the elements cannot be counted. Actually this community cannot be placed before me as a multiplicity formed of juxtaposed unities. To suppose such a multiplicity is to make it extraneous to me, to disrupt the whole intimacy between it and me. Now, it is precisely this intimacy that I have to account for.

To the extent that there cannot be a question of multiplicity, there can no more be a question of an element. Nevertheless, I agree that I am running into open contradiction, since I have spoken of a distribution *between*. This seems to actually suppose some calculable elements or marked-off zones.

Everything contrives to make me have recourse to an inadequate metaphor for interpreting a reality that I can only *intend*. I then turn to this metaphor or against it in order to disclose its inadequacy. Still an obscurity here. We look back *from* . . . ; therefore, it seems, from something reached or possessed and not simply intended.

What strikes me at the moment is the fact that what I am trying so painfully to elucidate corresponds to the Latin word *conscius*, taken in its etymological meaning. It is of my essence, in so far as I am conscious, to be associated with or joined to.

Montana, Christmas, 1940

This morning my thought came to dwell on the act of commemoration. We must eventually come to consider the act ambiguous that is expressed in the verb "to commemorate." Surely it is not merely a matter of a subjective recall, but of a re-creation, of a renewal. This is true of the religious feasts; with regard to the civil holidays, it is true only by analogy with the former. What I wrote two or three days ago on the subject of periodicity is here borne out and verified. Alain actually saw this but perhaps not thoroughly. The human condition is unthinkable without a periodic recurrence within the self or outside the self. But at the same time there passes through his recurrence something irreversible. We must try to make intelligible the relation which links recurrence with irreversibility. Does there exist here a pure and simple opposition? I cannot believe there is. An important question for one who wants to think about immortality. The periodicity appears to us as relative with respect to something that transcends it; but is that perhaps only an appearance necessary to let the creature apprehend itself as a creature? This is not perfectly clear in my mind; but I feel that there is a path to be followed.

Montana, December 31, 1940

That news unexpectedly received on Friday of my assignment to the Lyceum of Montpellier—how long has it intellectually paralysed me?

Yesterday evening this simple remark occurred to me: a Nietzsche, a Malraux believed that the man liberated from God would on that account rise in stat-

ure. He would have more room in some way. Everything conspires to let me think that the truth is quite
the opposite. I shall say as much in what concerns the
earthly life as that beyond. It is an extravagant illusion
to think that the earthly life is augmented when we
deny it all prolongation beyond the grave. Far from
finding an expansion there, man and life miserably
wither away. We must try and understand why. Basically we must revive Nietzsche's statement: Man is
something which ought to be transcended, but by
showing that in *Zarathustra* this affirmation is interpreted in a grossly temporal sense which alters and
eventually annuls it. To be resumed in more favorable
circumstances.[1]

[1] Today this seems to me to be thoroughly contestable. It
may be questioned as to whether for Nietzsche the advent of
super-man should not on the contrary have been considered in
a non-temporal manner (Notes of 1958).

[1941]

Lyons, January 2, 1941, in the Evening

My intention is to give a course in Montpellier on Good and Evil, from a psychological, moral and metaphysical point of view.

Montpellier, January 22, 1941

I do not know if it will be possible for me to note down anything. My classes drain me completely; quite precisely, they act on me like vampires.

Montpellier, February 25, 1941

I would like to undertake a study of the right to judge. The idea of it came to me from thoughts on scorn touched upon in one of my classes.

I will assume first that the meaning of these words "right to judge" is perfectly clear. The right will be denied me—I shall have to deny myself the right—to judge an act, the context or the conditions of which I know nothing of. Or again, I shall uphold the principle that I cannot put myself in the place of Pierre upon whom I am called to pass a judgment; legally it will therefore be impossible for me to do so. Inversely, if it were possible(?) for me to put myself in Pierre's place, I am, it seems, in a position to judge him, to judge his conduct. What is this possibility and what is this judgment?

This possibility consists of elements of information that I have of Pierre, of the situation in which he is placed. I grant that, with these elements to start with, I can somehow substitute myself for him mentally; we are thus assured of the grounds for a kind of experimentation, the nature of which we must now define. It is a matter of suppressing mentally in me any exteriority in relation to Pierre's conduct, which should exclude the possibility for example of my condemnation of his conduct. (Let us note that it is in fact a question of condemnation rather than of approbation.) I grant that this exteriority—analogous to that of two figures which one compares—has actually been suppressed.

Suppose now I were to accept that I would have acted in Pierre's place as he did; from this I shall tend to conclude that I am not qualified to condemn him. But if, on the other hand, I am convinced(?) that in his situation I would have acted otherwise, I shall in all probability infer that I have the right to judge him.

Has this form of reasoning any value whatsoever? (I observe that we do not always know precisely what is this right to judge which I sometimes arrogate to myself and sometimes disclaim.) The simplest reflection shows that it has no value whatsoever.

1. In his place I would have done the same. However, this may be because I see in myself the same weaknesses that I perceive in him. Basically, I have been led to this one simple fact (a fact bearing on the possible, however odd that may seem). I would have done the same but I know that I would have been wrong. In other words, I retain with respect to myself

(as with respect to the other with whom I am mentally identical) my freedom of judgment. The fact that, being placed in the same circumstances as Pierre, I would almost certainly have acted as he did, does not constitute in my eyes a valid reason for exonerating this action.

2. In his place I would have acted otherwise. Reflection at once shows me that this affirmation contains a dubious element. What does "in his place" mean? Is it not that I objectify unduly conditions which can be dissociated only by abstracting from the being who is placed in them? I suppose or I admit "that while being in his place" I would have remained myself exactly as I know myself; but is it not precisely this which is in question? In order to put myself in his place, would I not have to enter into his whole past, to take on somehow his vital graph? But if I were to achieve that, would I still be myself?

What am I to conclude? Simply, it seems, that the positive or negative result of the ideal experience by which I try to replace the other in order to establish if in the same circumstances I would have acted as he did, should not intervene in my judgment of this action. The reason is first that in the final analysis this experience is impracticable. Moreover, it is of my essence as a thinking being to be able to adopt a purely objective attitude with respect to my own acts.

However something deep within me, disputes the validity of this power, which I accord to my reason, to form valid judgments on an act, whether committed by me or by another, without troubling myself to find out what my own conduct would be, or again where I accept, at times absolutely ratify, the disagreement, the inconsistency between my judgments and my acts. Something in me protests against this kind of facility which my reason bestows on itself, by not taking into account my real conduct. It would be necessary to elucidate the meaning of this protestation. Could I not interpret it in more or less the following manner? My reason is after all still myself; it is not a supreme tribunal which, one knows neither why nor how, would come and take its seat within me or, if need be, pronounce judgment on my behalf, without such judgment basically effecting any change in what I do or what I am.

Montpellier, February 27, 1941

Perhaps all this is clarified by recalling a closely related example of what is meant by *the right to complain.* I have rented a house from someone who has warned me that the roof was in a state of disrepair and that it was in danger of giving way at the first bad weather. As a matter of fact the rooms are flooded, the furniture which I brought is damaged, etc. . . . You tell me that I do not have the right to complain, because I was warned. I took the risk. The owner does not deserve reproach at all. (Perhaps he was wrong in not having his roof repaired when he could have, but I agreed not to make an issue of this possible negligence.) To complain would be to accomplish a determinate act; it would be perhaps to start a lawsuit for damages, interests, etc. It is this action which I have previously withdrawn the right to bring into effect. In return, I retain the right—however, does this word have a precise meaning?—to judge severely the negligence of which the owner has given proof, and perhaps also my own carelessness. But this judgment remains essentially Platonic; it does not affect the real world; it remains purely ideal. After a manner of speaking, it is as though it were not. It is certainly impossible to see how one could deny me the right(?) to proceed to this reflection. . . . But here the term "reflection" brings with it a light. No thing, nor any person, in the world can refuse me the right to reflect. But precisely because the right is absolute and indefeasible, perhaps it might not be a right. It is indeed of the essence of a right that it can be recognized and safeguarded from without. Here, nothing similar. . . . Everything takes place within me and in an inviolable enclosure, which does not mean that, in fact, I cannot be put in a situation where it becomes impossible to reflect.

Notes of December, 1958

I am afraid I did not evaluate the bearing of this last reservation when I wrote these lines in 1941. Unfortunately, since then it has become increasingly clear that it is within men's power practically to abolish conscience. Nevertheless, the distinction indicated above retains some value, but this value is far from being absolute.

The tragedy of judgment is that, on the one hand, it implies a *stretching forth,* such as the tendency to think, "If I really judge, it is no longer I who judge." But on the other hand, in as much as the judgment is an act, it involves me and I must consequently bear the responsibility for it.

The notes that we are now about to read are related to a central question which has never ceased to haunt me. It is perhaps useful first to define its terms. Some phenomenologists like Heidegger and Jean-Paul Sartre, a great poet like Rainer Maria Rilke, are preoccupied with understanding the intimate link which binds me to my own death. Heidegger in particular transposes on the philosophical plane a theme admirably developed in the *Notebooks of Malte Laurid Brigge.* In so doing, he believed he could define as the invariant of the human condition what he calls being-toward-death, that is, in some way, the preordination which binds each one of us to his own death. Jean-Paul Sartre, in *Being and Nothingness,* has presented a critique of this conception which seems pertinent. But neither of these two philosophers seems to be seriously concerned to find out how the death of a loved being can metaphysically affect the one whom this death ravages. Deep down we may wonder whether these two thinkers, in spite of their professions of realism, have directed their attention sufficiently to the nature of the link which unites the lover with the beloved. We may wonder if in fact they do not remain prisoners of a destructive idealism, which they have theoretically overcome.

We are going to examine the reflections that center round this problem of the death of the loved being and its implications.

[1942]

Le Peuch, May 19, 1942

For the past few days—and even fur-
ther back, since always—I have been dwelling linger-
ingly upon ideas well-nigh beyond my grasp. I would
like to see them bodied forth. I think I will have
accomplished my mission on earth only when I shall
have succeeded in doing so.

To survive. . . . In what sense can I say: I have
survived such a person? This affirmation seems to make
sense only in terms of a certain representation, that of a
distance covered. Such a person and I have travelled
together until such a moment, that is, up to such a
point. From there on I did the journey alone. Such a
person did not accompany me beyond that point. To
survive is therefore to bypass (someone) on a certain
road. I represent my past life along a road which "I go
over with my eyes" as I turn back toward it. Along this
road which stretches out under my eyes and even behind me, I mark the places where lie motionless, one
after the other, all those whom I have survived and
bypassed, just as I myself will one day be.

But it is necessary to fix my thought on this immobil-
ization. It is not true that these beings, who *were* at
least and perhaps still *are* living just as I myself am,

have been immobilized in those places. As a matter of fact, it is I who immobilize them, by a movement of imagination as irrepressible as the one which is exercised on persons whom I have loved more. This is why my imagination is fascinated by the last look which these persons have permitted me of themselves, by the last conversations which we have had. These gazes and these conversations are not, like the looks and conversations that preceded them, drawn into a certain movement, into a gradual falling away of life. They tend to present themselves to me as endowed with a true power to stop. They seem to bring out for me the closed opacity of a thing. I knock against them as one bumps into a closed door. Nevertheless, I repeat, reflection always shows me that there exists here an effect of imagination from which the very same, or perhaps a superior, imagination must allow me to liberate myself.

Fundamentally I set out from an assumption that is well-nigh impossible to formulate. The assumption is that my friend has remained in the state in which I saw him, on that hospital bed where I eavesdropped on the words that punctuated his agony. I did so in the same manner as I could answer the question, "Where have you left your companion? Where was he when he stopped walking?" I might be able to reply: "He was at the edge of a grove; he was so tired that he must still be there."

The question that I ask myself is: to what extent is a life—my friend's or mine—really comparable to a similar distance covered?

If I consider my friend like some body occupying at every instant a determinate place in space, the comparison has some meaning. In other words, the body moved; it is carried here and there while in the meantime it was undergoing an infinity of internal transfor-

mations. It is the same with my body. It is also true
that each of us has had to cover a certain distance in
the strictly spatial meaning of that word. It is true that
I saw him for the last time, that I left him in that
hospital room. Shall I say later, at the cemetery, it was
no longer he, it was an image? Shall I say that my road
companion has fallen in this place where I still see him?
But in so doing I clearly indicate that it is impossible
for me to think of my companion and the body as not
being anything but one, since this body is for me nothing but an empty cover, at least when life has withdrawn from it. (This mode of expression has a certain
drawback. It seems to imply a dualistic spiritualism
which probably does not cover human experience
grasped in its reality. What is to be kept in mind here
simply is that the history of my companion—let us say
more precisely his visible history—stops short on this
side of a material development which has no bearing
except on a thing.)

As I indicated previously, the more I have loved a
person, the less I shall succeed in freeing myself from
the haunting memory which lingers on his last state; or
rather, this fascination for last memories, for the last
places, is the very manifestation of a love, the character
of which still remains to be defined.

But at the same time—and there lies the paradox on
which I wish to concentrate my thought—what somehow measures my friendship, my tenderness, is the
depth of a past which should obliterate these last memories; for if I am in good faith and of even disposition, I
shall discover in them the testimony of an effacement
rather than of a presence. Hence the paradox that the
memory to which my affliction clings, as though it had
retained the most precious fragments of a departed
person, is after all, I am forced to agree, that in which

he would be least recognized, an utter stranger to what he was.

That is not all. When I become fixated on the image of the distance gone or of the interrupted course, I seem to treat the other as though he had been left on the hither side of a goal which I myself have reached, or which I still have the hope or pretentiousness of reaching. By the same token, I unduly apply to the other's life a standard which is perhaps mine—that is still not certain—but which this life assuredly does not admit of. What is the proof for this? The seemingly undeniable fact that the more fully I see myself, the more I am (the more I have the awareness of being), and the less I see myself as being *en route to*.[1] A distance run is only for the sake of and by way of representation; and the most genuinely, the most passionately, lived life is the one which does not experience the need, and doubtless does not recognize the possibility, of being represented to itself.

Le Peuch, May 20, 1942

While reflecting on the fascinating power of last memories, I observe that it is certainly due to the fact that the *still* and the *no longer* are joined to it to the point of being indistinguishable. He was still there, and yet already he no longer was, as though in place of the person's presence I put back the absence that was going to be his, embody him in itself. I wonder if the essence of the phantom would not consist in this embodied absence within a presence which already is no more than an appearance. The unvarying quality of the

[1] This expression would call for differentiation in shades of meaning.

phantom: it can no longer change precisely because it is pure aspect of a pure absence.

I shall, however, refrain from claiming that the phantom may be nothing other than this last memory picture: all that I can see is that my experience furnishes me with at least the counterpart, and perhaps the source, of this memory picture. There will, however, be one great difficulty to resolve, that of understanding how a phantom can be given to many a consciousness, and not just to one. Must we admit that this last look, considered this time from the point of view of the subject, may have an immobilizing, that is an obsessive, power for the very one who has contemplated it, and not only for the one to whom it has been proposed? The expression here is ambiguous. I have not succeeded in formulating clearly the distinction between the representation seen by the person who is going to die, and that which he gives of himself to those who are going to survive him. . . .

Le Peuch, May 31, 1942

I have just re-read these notes, and I seem to feel the throb of a new-born idea in them. I have not written anything more charged with experience, that's for sure.

I always come back to the image of a distance run. It is also from this point of view that the word "lose" takes its meaning. We were together; I lost him (as one loses a child in a crowd). He has merged. . . .

Merged? . . . But with what? There is surely room for equivocation here. Actually I have a tendency to conjure up in my mind, in spite of myself, the dissemination of physical elements of what I call "being."

> They have melted away into deep oblivion;
> The red clay has swallowed up the white.

But I feel strongly the existence of a temptation; these elements have retained nothing of the being whom I survive and whom I mourn. *Excreta* was Schopenhauer's word (for them). In a sense they are really that. But we must go beyond this meaning if we believe in the resurrection of the body; however, that should not intervene at this point of the analysis.

I think it is necessary to pay close attention to the relation between this being, this "thou," and myself; it is the means of arming oneself against the temptation to objectify by asking what has become of "this thing." (To this question, and to it alone, the answer would be, it has disintegrated, it has been dissolved.) The being who remains present to my thought, to my heart, to my inner vision, has not at all been dissolved. There is a separation between the image of the thing and the changes it undergoes, on the one hand, and the inner vision of the being rooted in its mysterious permanence on the other. I must wonder how universal thought resolves, or thinks of resolving, this contradiction; next take this solution in hand by making explicit the assumptions on which it is based. Recently I wrote to P. H. on the occasion of the anniversary of the death of his wife, "I understand more and more clearly that the word 'lost' does not make sense." At that time I referred precisely to this experience of a maintained presence. But there is the other danger, the one which I have pointed out many a time, the danger of being hypnotized, of being fixated on an image, of obsession. What I perceived this morning is that my relation to the other ought to triumph over this obsession; for, after all, we are concerned primarily with *the life of this relation*. Let us observe, moreover, that the word "relation" is probably inadequate here, for I represent as a relation what is first lived in some other way, as an exchange, as a living communication. The question still remains whether it is possible in some way to reach the "*in itself*" of the other outside of this exchange or this communication.

But the very manner in which I have expressed myself in recalling the life of a relation excludes every materialistic representation of a memory. Now there exists in each of us an almost invincible tendency to equate memories which I have retained of the other with photographs that I might have kept in my possession and which I could glance over. "I think of" would mean: "I have taken in hand one of these photographs." From this point of view the idea of a living relation to . . . loses all significance. My thoughts of May 19 permit me to see that I can adopt a large variety of inner attitudes with respect to the departed one; I am even capable of a certain interior activity with regard to him. The method of research that I would have in mind would consist in asking whether we cannot proceed from this activity to a "communication with," or, more precisely, on what conditions this transition could be conceived. These investigations take on a meaning, and even become possible, only on one preliminary condition. That condition is to recognize that the other is in no way here reducible to an image, to a representation which I might have in my possession, which I could handle at will, but which of course would be entirely passive in my hands. If that were so, it is very clear that the very idea of a communication would have to be regarded as devoid of meaning.

At this point, I shall make a digression. It seems beyond dispute that certain clairvoyants may have the power to put themselves in communication with an absent person by means of his photograph or portrait. It even seems that some of them possess the inexplicable power to say, at the mere appearance of this picture or portrait, whether the person is alive or not. This fact so strange, so disconcerting belongs to those facts from which the thought of the wise man or the philosopher turns away, as it were instinctively, because it tends to shatter the categories of all empirical or rational knowledge. For my part, this rejection constitutes a kind of philosophical sin. On the contrary I think it would be of the greatest importance to examine the conditions that make such a grasp of consciousness possible. It must be granted, however paradoxical that may seem, that the image, photographic or otherwise, ought to be able to be considered not only as a distinct object, but as somehow being an integral part of the one whom it represents and as still participating in his life. The privilege of the clairvoyant would consist in grasping this non-objective being of the image, which behaves with respect to him as an active center, instead of being just an inert thing.

I do not in any way conceal the hazardous element in such considerations, nor the bewildering quality of the paradoxes to which they lead. But I think it can be beneficial in every way to widen a little the breach in the armor of intelligibility under which we suffocate more and more each day. Nor do I conceal any more the fact that a hypothesis, like the one I have just outlined, can appear to arise from the pre-logical mentality described by Lévy-Bruhl and his disciples. However, we may ask ourselves whether these sociologists have at all suspected the metaphysical problem which the very existence of such a mentality supposes. For it is important to find out whether, in breaking away—not completely but to a great extent—from this mentality and from these categories, man has not become increasingly blind to certain fundamental aspects of the world in which he has been privileged to live. This possibility, vaguely seen by Bergson, does not seem to have been seriously explored by the philosophers who followed him, this for reasons not difficult to discern. To explore, for sure: here research takes on an speleological character. It has to do with opening up a road at the bottom of an abyss, in the flickering light of a reflection which owes to itself to question at each step the principles on which our everyday knowledge rests.

Impossible to forge further ahead along this way! I shall be satisfied with the remark that even where superficial observation discovers a simple relation of being to image, the latter overlays perhaps an infinitely more hidden relation of being to being.

It must be pointed out, however, that here reflection is in danger of being immobilized by the projections of a materialistic imagination. Am I not in fact perilously exposed to represent the Other as a thing which, before being dissolved, has permeated some of his expressions with a mysterious quality which survives for a while this dissolution? That, from all evidence, is the height of absurdity. If such a permeation is conceivable, it is in so far as it is exercised on a thing. What is in question here is not at all the image in so far as it is a thing (for example, a photographic object having a given dimension, thickness, texture), but in so far as it is representational. We might almost say that what is at stake is the soul of the image and not its body.

I ought therefore to resist, with all my power, the temptation to interpret as a physical modification what can only be a participation belonging to an entirely different order. Besides, it is very clear that, in the very attempt to represent this participation, I materialize it and fall into the error which has just been denounced. All that becomes a little clear if we consider that what I call a photograph takes on life and reality only through a certain *interior* light which makes what in itself is only a blob of color appear as a face, or as a being with expression. The two terms to be reconciled are not therefore in the least two things, one of which would be a being and the other its image. They are rather a combination of spiritual forces through which this being is maintained in existence on the one hand, and on the other, the act, equally spiritual, by which it is given to a subject to apprehend this being from the outside as a distinct and visible individuality. We must bring outselves to see, however difficult that may be, that in considering this individuality through some medium or go-between, of whatever sort, we make our own in some degree the powers that are immanent in it. The truth is that what presents itself from a certain perspective as something apprehended or grasped can from a complementary perspective be regarded as an appearance and as a giving of itself. This is perhaps somewhat easier to understand in the case of a portrait, in the pictorial meaning of the word, than in the case of a simple photograph. In some way, the model truly gives himself to the painter, provided at least that the latter is a genuine portrait painter and is not simply looking for a pretext to enable him to sketch some forms. The painter has therefore not succeeded in giving a resembling and profoundly significant image of the model unless he has been in sympathy—in the deepest meaning of that word—with the inner, sustained impulse whereby the other presents himself to his peers as a visible person, as this particular person and not that other. Now it is quite obvious that there would be no sense in imagining the impregnation of the painting by some kind of fluid flowing from the original.

But a formidable difficulty still exists and it is of the

utmost honesty to admit it. It has to do with the clairvoyant who claims to know whether the portrait model is actually living or not. How are we to conceive that, by installing himself, if we may say so, at the heart of the inner development of the absent person, conjured up through the mediation of the image, he may be able to recognize if there exists as actual or completed duration? Perhaps, however, the difficulty accrues from the fact that, despite ourselves, we picture this concrete duration as an essence which would be grasped in a non-temporal manner. But if it is really a duration which we are dealing with, one can perhaps imagine that there may be room in the clairvoyant for the feeling of a harmony or disharmony between the awareness he has of his own actual duration and that which he has of the other's duration.

There comes to my mind an image which, if it were adopted and utilized as a means of elucidation, could only augment the difficulty in which we are placed. It is the image of a melody which I pick up through a written or printed notation. I make it mine; I live it. But it is quite obvious that there would be no point in raising a problem of time with respect to it, as it is placed outside of all reference to a determinate moment of time. For such a reference to be able to intervene, it is necessary that there come into play a prophetic sympathy of an entirely different order. We may observe, moreover, that the notation which serves as a point of departure is a method external to the recorded melody; whereas we have seen that the portrait can to a degree be envisaged as a mode of existence of the being who has served as a model for it. Beginning with the notation, I construct a certain form; I make it exist. But in the latter case, nothing of the kind is to be found: clairvoyance is exactly the opposite of such a construc-

tion, since it renders itself sufficiently open to let itself
be magnetized by a certain presence, or again to hollow
itself out in order to receive what is brought to it. The
image which occurs to the mind is that of an irruption
or of a tide. But how are we to understand that for the
clairvoyant there may be a difference of quality that is
felt between the onrush of a continuing duration and
that of a completed duration? Is this not a contradiction in terms? How could that which no longer is
overrun us? But it seems that we are really dealing here
with two irreducible modalities of existence, let us say
perhaps an arrested existence and an existence in progress. It would be preferable, then, to substitute the
words "overrunning" or "invasion" for that of "irruption": a harbor can be overrun by ice.

No matter how obscure and uncertain these remarks
may be, however doubtful even the possibilities they set
out to clarify, they seem to me to have this great
advantage of forcing the mind to break with all objective (better to say objectifying) representation of life
and death. The existence of the deceased ceases to be
regarded as the existence of a thing which has fallen
apart or of a machine that has broken down. By bringing in for example the notion of arrested existence, I
am perhaps prepared to conceive more concretely and
more metaphysically that of a suspended existence
without my yet being in any position at all to say what
this suspense announces or perhaps prepares. Nevertheless, on this plane, it becomes possible for me to imagine how I could perhaps *conspire* with this existence in
expectation in terms of a certain recollection or fervent
attention which is already perhaps the beginning of
prayer.

However, we should not underestimate the value of
the objections we might run into by expressing our-

selves in this fashion. One might ask: Is not this arrested existence in contrast to an existence in progress,
that of a thing, of an object as such? Consequently, is
there not something fraudulent in attributing to it
suspense, slumber, or even the state of the chrysalis
which prepares for its ultimate transmutations? But we
must immediately reply that clairvoyance can never be
anything but intersubjective and that it is probably
absurd to imagine that a thing as thing may be able to
set it in motion or merely permit it. This would be
supplemented by the remarks on psychometry which I
previously hazarded in the *Metaphysical Journal.*

In short, it is a matter of prospecting and clearing,
through all these winding and adventurous paths, a
ground on which the mystery which is attached to the
death of the other can be finally, I do not say elucidated, but at least confronted. One can never say sufficiently how much this clearance is necessary for beings
who are as much the prisoners of images borrowed from
the technical world as ourselves. It is only by roundabout ways and by means of expedients, at least at the
beginning, that we can hope to escape from the prison
in which despair lies in wait for us at every corner.

On what conditions is it conceivable that the being
whom I have lost, or whom I imagine or am supposed
to have lost, may yet have a part in me and in my life?

The being whom I have lost: but we lose only what
we possessed. Was this other mine? In what sense? Is
my companion mine? He is with me; that is his way of
being mine. If it had been true to say that I had him, is
it precise to say that I have him no more? Or on the
contrary is it my imagination which exercises its maleficent activity and persuades me of it? It is very clear that
the formidable problem of ipseity is involved in all this

search. Necessity to state for particular beings the problem which philosophers have in a general way reserved to the speculation on God.

The primary investigation must therefore be on the idea of real loss. Perhaps—this is only a shot in the dark—this idea is all the more applicable as it is more strictly brought to bear on the possessed. I can in all truth lose the object I possess. This watch which I touched, which I felt as mine is no longer there; it has fallen down, someone has taken it, or I have lost it. Whence perhaps this conclusion (rather hasty, but which it is necessary to note): to the degree that I think I possessed the other I can truly be aware of having lost him. This is why it is often so true to say that so and so has lost his child. But immediately there is a difficulty, a complication: it can appear that what I do not possess is by definition alien to me and I cannot really lose what has never been mine. It would therefore be necessary to get to explore this middle region which is that of the "with" (and which Sartre has so strangely misunderstood).

What I see for the moment is that what I have written about obsession is surely linked up with possession. By letting myself be obsessed by the last state or the last image, I transform the being I love into a thing which in effect turns out to be lost. With this thing I could not form a veritable "we"; and if there is an indestructibility, it is only by starting from the "we" that I can succeed in thinking about it.

That however is only a beginning. It would be necessary to show now that it is in the order of having that the opposition between the image and the thing itself (*res ipsa*) is most fatal. The emphasis is all the more strongly placed on the disappearance of the thing as the latter is more experienced or claimed as mine. The thing is no longer there. There exists here a veritable tension between reality and subjectivity. I mean that the reality of the missing object is all the more painfully felt and remembered as this thing has become more a part of myself, and as I have more eagerly appropriated it to myself. The pain in this case is a lesion in the strongest sense of the word. I suffer for myself and in myself. But the suffering, like love itself, has another pole in as much as it is suffering for the sake of the other (for his own sake).

Perhaps it may not be out of place to perceive that the more the missing being is really conceived as being (but what does that actually mean?), the less will it be grasped as possession; the less, consequently, will its disappearance be felt as a loss. [Unfortunately it is necessary to add that all our affections are possessive, a fact which appreciably limits the practical bearing of this observation.]

Before probing deeper, I observe once more that in this order the inner attitude is determining: it profoundly affects what we wrongly call the object itself, instead of being merely contingent as when we are simply dealing with things which passively follow their destiny as things. I am therefore right, at least in principle, to presume that my inner attitude with respect to the one who is no longer there has an effect upon him (in as much as he stands in relation to me, but this relation has a constitutive and not an exterior quality if the other has been truly *with* me). It is therefore not a matter of indifference that I am hypnotized by him as by a lost possession. Thereby I actually betray him. [I mean that I cease to think of him as a being and that I tend to treat him as an object.] However, there comes into play a dialectic of betrayal; I can have the impression of betraying the other in detaching my thought from his final state, for instance from the excruciating pains he underwent before dying. Then I allow myself to be hypnotized by the idea that such a detachment is based on indifference. Nevertheless it is really out of love for the other that I must free myself from this obsession. I owe it to him not to immobilize him, not to deny him as it were being and life.

I also see, in a most general way, that I falsify everything by confusing the being with the memories I have of him, and by treating these latter as idols, or if one prefers as relics, in transferring for example onto these memories themselves the fondness I have for this being. Here as always there is a transcendence to be preserved. What is it exactly?

It seems that the more a being has been recognized, greeted by me in his essence as being, the less he is in fact confused with the details views that circumstances have permitted me to see of him; the more in fact I have been able to recognize his value, that is to say, something that can be illustrated only within experience, but which goes infinitely beyond these illustrations. I have said "value." Another way to describe it would be "essence." However, we would do well to guard ourselves against the temptation to objectify. Let us remember that it is here a question of a relational life. What interests us is to know what the bond between the other and me has been; out of what so to say has this bond been forged? [Today I would be inclined to put the strongest emphasis on the credit which I have opened in the other's name, that is to say, on the hope that animated my relation to him, hope tending toward an ever closer communion.]

It is perhaps possible to recognize dimly that this personal sorrow which is linked to his disappearance is a necessary moment precisely in this that I have to triumph over it (as hope triumphs over despair, or more precisely over the temptation to despair). I must moreover keep myself from making false connections here. This sorrow is not the act of what I have called the "self I" (*moi je*), in as much as this sorrow does not involve any claim; but what is true is that this sorrow is essentially of the flesh. In as much as we are fleshly beings, we cannot, nor even must we, wish anything but that this sorrow be spared to us. That is, I believe, actually the only authentic foundation for a higher relation between the living and the dead. In short, I owe it to "him" not to abandon myself to this obsession in which someone would say that I tend to bury both of us completely. Everything happens as though the other could triumph over it only on condition that I triumph over it first. But once again I can triumph over it only through my love for him. There is nothing common between such a sentiment and the egoism of the one who tries to dispel his feeling of sadness, that is, to distract himself. The other is present in the act by which I liberate myself not from him, but from the idol I substituted for him in making him static.

Here we again come across the problem of ipseity. What do I mean—and how can I be sure of being within my rights—when I affirm that "it is really he," that it is his very self that is present in this act? Here one should show that in spite of everything we remain obsessed with the idea of communication in the physical order, of a wire connecting two stations. The question "Is he there in person?" presents itself to us in the form "Is it he who is at the other end of the wire?" or "Is it someone else?"; or "In the last analysis could it be that there is no one, while things happen as though there were someone?" I note here in passing a thought that has often occurred to me: our inventions seem called to furnish more and more precise metaphors to serve us as aids when we attempt to conceive that is really beyond every conceivable metaphor and technique. This problem of ipseity is not truly separable from another question and we experience some difficulty in stating it in intelligible terms. We wonder "Is someone there? Who is there?" But what does "to be there" mean? The "being there" does not allow itself to be separated from an *elsewhere* whence someone may come; the "in person" does not let itself be separated from the idea of a possible delegation: he did not come himself, but he sent someone in his place. The objection which a certain realism of common sense opposes to every one of these inquiries, which of course would have to be implied in every serious examination of spiritism, is that he is no longer anywhere, since he is no longer at all. But to this realism it is important to reply that the *he* about whom I anxiously question myself, that is, the being I invoke and whose perpetuated presence is indispensable to me, that *he* who is in reality a *thou* would not have been confused with the *he* who is only a thing, a thing which has disintegrated, which has fallen apart. The experience of which we are speaking can be translated only by an "it is you," a "here you are," an "is it really you?" This experience is situated, in spite of appearances, outside the world to which everything that can be treated as a thing belongs.

[1943]

Le Peuch, January 23, 1943

First notes for a course on fatherhood which was requested for Lyons. Fatherhood as Heading—Fatherhood as a value of exaltation: "I am a father!" . . . Pride.

Take into account adoption, on the one hand, and loss of parental rights on the other, in order to show that it is impossible to reduce fatherhood to a biological category, and yet it belongs to the flesh. Adoption is a grafting.

What is it to beget? Difference between giving and producing. Thus it is possible to understand why fatherhood is not reduced to a mode of causality.

Le Peuch, January 24, 1943

Symmetry of the positions on evil and death. So far as it is my end, death does not admit a beyond and it cannot be transcended. By the same token, however, it merges with evil. Death as thought is opposed to death as felt; it is by contrast directly transcended. This means that it is made to vanish. A third position is necessary—the same for evil.

Pessimism, applicable to a world in which death is

apprehended as a process; but it is precisely as unlike a process that death appears in the sacrifice.

Immortality, conceivable only within a world where sacrifice is not merely possible but actually accomplished. The passage from one dimension to the other.

Le Peuch, February 17, 1943

Continuation of Notes on Fatherhood. There is a sense in which fatherhood appears purely and simply as a blood relationship between two persons. But this supposes that they are treated as given; now it is precisely from this point of view that the notion of fatherhood is empty of its authentic meaning. The more we persist in interpreting fatherhood as a relation between beings given separately the less can we understand what it is.

Le Peuch, February 18

I wondered yesterday if it would not be advisable to question the metaphysical foundation of paternal authority: to investigate in what conditions, in what context of *unbelief* the latter is obliterated (in relation to Robert de Traz's very fine novel, *The Shadow and the Sun*), and disappears where the father-son relation is not interpreted in the light of the relation between creator and creature.

Indissoluble bond between acting and being acted upon within fatherhood.

Embarrassment of the father in the presence of the son and of the son in the presence of the father. Whence does it arise? To me it seems to be linked to the feeling of intrusion where the relation between the

child and the mother is too intimate. (No need to
bring in the Freudian categories here.)

Paternal authority is linked to the consciousness of a
responsibility; both disappear at the same time. This is
a clue. For the feeling of responsibility is eliminated
where procreation comes about either by chance or as
an extension of a simple sensual whim. On the other
hand, it cannot and should not be the result or effect of
a calculating will.

I always come back to the outpouring arising out of a
lived fullness: the link with marriage understood in its
true character.

In short, start from the analysis of the lived situation
of the father in the presence of the child: see how this
situation can be distorted (either if I am aware of not
having anything to do myself with this child's presence
in the world, or if on the contrary I treat him as my
work, as the effect of my will). In both cases one
falsifies a relation which can be grasped only with extreme difficulty and which has the characteristic that it
involves an appeal.

Le Peuch, February 19

In short, this is the situation which must be understood in its fullness, with the values that it can involve
but does not necessarily involve. Paternity is a certain
"being in the presence of. . . ."

One might say that after all we actually have here a
verifiable relation, something that ought to be able to
be proved or rejected. This is absolutely certain, but
this relation would not suffice to define paternity in the
true and full meaning of the word. As always, it is
necessary "to dramatize": I am in the presence of a
child, I know that this child is mine, or more exactly I

can say that in all probability this child is really mine. Let us grant that this is given to my consciousness outside of all affectivity. I *know*, to the extent that this word can have a meaning here, that I am the father of this child. But this certitude does not awaken any echo in me. I do not feel that I am the father. I recognize that I have some obligations toward this little creature, because "it is normal that a father," but nothing more. It can happen that this little being appears to me as an intruder, as someone who comes unexpectedly to trouble my life or our life. It can happen also that by putting myself in his place I deplore his position: would it not be better for him if he remained in Limbo? And these thoughts develop outside of the kind of sanctuary in which the word "fatherhood" gets its true meaning; these are profane thoughts but they will appear so only after I have entered the sanctuary. This word is really one that is fitting, for fatherhood is a mode of piety. And we should be able to speak of paternal piety just as we speak of filial piety.

Now how does the situation become transformed when I am in the sanctuary? At this point we must take into account the remarks of yesterday. Negatively, let us say that the little child no longer appears to me either like myself or like a stranger (unwanted and one who would be in short the fruit of a misunderstanding, the expression of a breach of trust, and whose life would be guilty of an offense against me). There is first the respect, the profound emotion, in the presence of a being independent of me and of the staggering unknown concealed by him. But this sentiment I could strictly speaking experience in the presence of any small child. There is more to it: this little child is mine. What does the possessive mean here? To be sure, it can mean: he belongs to me. But, on reflection, this will have to appear to me as a pure aberration. For it is clear that these words do not have any meaning whatever. What is really true instead is that he has an infinite claim upon me, and the more I grasp the tragic and unfathomable character of existence, the more I shall recognize that this is the truth. It is as though he said: "By what right did you draw me out of the night, did you awaken me to this awful world?" True, I can then be tempted to reply to this accusation: "I did not want it; you were born in spite of me, in spite of us; truly we did not know what we were doing; we ourselves have been caught in the snare of life. In these conditions we have only to do the best we can, to find a compromise which may not be too onerous either for you or for us." I note in passing that this specious manner of arguing, conceivable in man is barely conceivable in woman. And yet, a profound perversion is possible whereby the woman joins in this kind of surfeited protest. But all this is possible only outside the sanctuary. Within the sanctuary, the child's claim on me, far from being a motive of hate, becomes on the contrary a reason for love. "I love you because of all that you expect of me." Here, however, a new perversion is possible: I am in danger of becoming attached to you to the degree in which you will incarnate the trouble which I would have to give myself to bring you up. There is a grave danger there.

In reality, it is not a question of making but only of permitting you to become what you are, and this is precisely independent of what I am. I would recognize that all the more profoundly as I would the better gauge my insufficiency, my imperfection. Here again, a snare is possible: the idea of a second chance, to attain with you, through you, what I could not realize by myself.

The sanctuary is first of all the forgetting of myself, the forgetting both of what I am and of what I am not, of what I have attained and what I have not been able to attain.

But a new danger lies in wait for me: total effacement before you; thereby I am in danger of making you an egoist. It is in your interest that I let you, in spite of all, recognize what you owe me.

Le Peuch, February 20

It is necessary to be aware of a certain confusion which lies at the root of the crisis of paternal authority; the origins of this crisis are at bottom the same as those of the crisis of the birth-rate. I must return to the ideas expressed last year that there is a nuptial bond between man and life. The less life appears as a gift the worse this crisis becomes: by what right have I inflicted life on this creature who did not ask for existence? I must show perhaps why the question does not arise in the same terms for the woman who also is in some degree a victim: she suffers and her very suffering creates between her and the child a bond which does not exist with the man. This suffering can in some way be embittered where woman is in secret or open revolt against her fate. But it often happens that the woman is reconciled to it as she feels living within her the being whom initially she might have wished to do away with.

The notion of gift is linked with that of value. The more life is conceived as an indifferent modality of existence which has no intrinsic value, the less it is apprehended as a gift. Pleasure will then appear as the sole possible justification for life. This could have two sorts of results: sometimes the child will be detested as a kill-joy, sometimes the kind of compassion that he inspires as a companion caught in the same predicament will degenerate into a sort of complicity. In any case, the idea of society will not play the slightest part here. From the phenomenological point of view which is mine, I believe that we would not be able to accord the least reality to sociological constructs in this domain.

In short, my investigation would be oriented in the following direction: disorder excludes the awareness of legitimate authority. This authority can be exercised only on the basis of a lived experience which can moreover be betrayed in the manner in which it is conceptualized (as in a certain traditionalism). But this lived experience cannot be reflected upon in its truth without uncovering certain assumptions that we must be aware of, assumptions in which is articulated a certain affirmation of life as reality and value.

Basically it is a question of reflecting upon and extirpating a certain nihilism which can manifest itself either as anarchic individualism, or as a totalitarianism in which the individual takes refuge in order to forget his nothingness, to turn away from his own non-being. I must show, as counterproof, that fatherhood tends to be abolished in one case as in the other. I must add that there exists here something much more fragile than in the relation between mother and child. Fatherhood is essentially vulnerable; its being can be attacked from within: the father's possible rancor against the son, the son's irritation and revolt against the father.

Le Peuch, February 22

From all this it follows that we wholly distort reality by distinguishing a sort of objective substrate which would be fatherhood properly so called, and a subjec-

tive attitude adopted by consciousness in relation to
this substrate and of which, at bottom, we could legitimately make abstraction. The truth is that this attitude
is on the contrary constitutive. The more we tend to
make the biological data and considerations predomi-
nate, the more we tend to obliterate in man the meaning of fatherhood.

In this respect, the progress of biology can represent
an appalling danger for man. It is permissible to ask if
ignorance in this domain has not been in the past a true
blessing: it would for instance be infinitely perilous for
man to acquire control over the sex of his descendants.

Le Peuch, February 23

Today, on the road from Gondres, I reflected on
what I would like to call "teleology in reverse," that is,
the existence of a principle which would be oriented, as
toward its proper end, to the destruction of all positive
finality. One would radically misconstrue the nature of
this principle if he likened it to a pure mechanism. I
wonder if any disease whatsoever is intelligible without
the intervention of a maleficent principle of this kind.

Basically the pure maleficent is in us. It must therefore be also outside us, for there is no reason at all to
suppose any difference in nature between the forces
that are at work in us and in things. We ought to seek
in the name of what postulate we are loathe to admit
this similarity, or this identity, and also to minimize or
to deny the pure maleficent. We shall take this up
again and go into it more deeply. At the same time it
will be necessary to see later on in what conditions this
teleology in reverse can be admitted without adhering
thereby to a Manichean metaphysics.

Le Peuch, February 24

During my walk to Cavagnac this afternoon, my
ideas of yesterday have scarcely become clearer. I believe that I see the necessity of rendering more precise
the attitudes of contemporary thought with respect to
the idea of a radical evil. It seems to me that it is rather
on these attitudes than on the principle that I must
reflect.

Le Peuch, March 3

Father M. asks me to share with him some thoughts
on the responsibilities of a Catholicism that has strayed
and lost its virility and which some writers denounce
(Montherlant, I think, Petitjean and others). He re-
quests me especially to share with him some thoughts
on the role which a certain notion of sin can play.

This loss of virility seems to consist above all in the
weakening of the sense of risk and in the obliteration of
the sense of the "city." (Is there any link between these
two phenomena?) It is necessary, I think, to find out
what kind of alteration in the sense of sin can contribute to this weakening. A first point seems obvious: the
more sin is conceived in terms of the individual that I
am the more I will be in danger of becoming isolated
from the community—a false detachment. It is necessary to feel united with all men in sin. The notion of
sin as a principle of communion.

The sense of sin differs entirely from the feeling of
imperfection. It is inseparable from the sentiment of
divine Love.

The feeling of imperfection, the nature of which
should also be elucidated, is ambiguous in its implica-

tions. Is not my imperfection due to a bad intrinsic quality, or to a lack of order, in the elements which constitute me? Or, on the contrary, do I have my share of
responsibility in this imperfection of my being? To be
sure, my sin is such—it is mine and it is sin—only if I
am truly involved in it. One could not, however, say
that it is my work, for it is to a true work what death is
to life, and if I say that it is a "work of death" I point
out the antinomy that it involves.

It seems that the reality of my sin does not touch my
conscience except to the degree that I awaken to the
infinite Love of which I am the object. But inversely if
this Love is not recognized by me, I am unable to look
upon myself as a sinner.

I note finally that this sin is not only mine but ours. I
cannot, without pharisaism, observe that *they* sin and
declare myself exempt from this sin. If the evil is in
them, I am inclined to affirm that it is also in me.
Perhaps by this indirect way I can better educate myself
to the notion of sin—by reporting, for example, the
repercussion which the others' sin has on me, the sentiments of hate, of vengeance, or envy which it inspires
in me. It is in this sense that there is a communion. If I
am not aware of communing with others in sin, I
cannot hope to commune with them in the experiences
which lead to salvation. All these observations seem
important to me.

Tomorrow I shall reflect on the relation between sin
and life, in particular within sexual relations. I must
distinguish between false and true asceticism. By taking
these inquiries as a point of departure, I can hope to
reply to the question put by Father M.

Strictly speaking is there a feeling of imperfection? I
acknowledge myself, I judge myself as imperfect. But

what is the kind of experience on which I base this judgment which I pronounce? One might perhaps be tempted to say that I confront myself such as I am, with a certain idealism more or less clearly conceived. But it is very doubtful that this interpretation is precise. It seems rather that my imperfection is experienced as an inhibition. I feel myself stopped on a certain road. There are some cases in which I have a clear picture of this road, others in which I am led to imagine such a particular act which would remain to be accomplished and of which I feel myself incapable. For instance, this money that I have just received I should give to N. He needs it, but I do not have the courage to give it; it would deprive me of a book or a trip that I like to make.

But it is quite necessary to observe that this ascertaining of a stop does not necessarily change into a judgment of imperfection; I am always inclined to find a justification for my abstention. The decisive movement will consist in setting aside this specious justification, in seeing through it. It would be better to give this amount to N.; however, I cannot resolve to do it. I recognize therefore that in such a particular case I fall short of what I ought to be. Is it by way of generalization or induction that I pass to the recognition of my overall imperfection? In reality a universal is apprehended through the particular experience: for me to behave in this fashion in such a particular case, I must. . . . I see myself through my act or my failure to act. But this imperfection is not yet apprehended as a sin. It can manifest itself to me as an infirmity, as a pure deficiency, almost as an observed inability on the physical plane, such as that of carrying a certain weight for a long time, of doing a certain exercise, etc.

Le Peuch, March 5

In order that my imperfection may appear to me as sin, it is necessary, but not sufficient, that I recognize myself responsible for it. But it is not enough: to say that this imperfection must be first localized for me in my own act of willing and this act of willing must appear to me, if not as radically bad, at least as divided. But this is only a preliminary condition. The "I see and approve the better things, I follow the worse" still does not translate a specific experience of sin; it is only an observation. But what I strongly feel, although still in a confused way, is that sin properly so called is not observed strictly speaking. Sin is not a fact, and if it is a given, then one must distinguish between a given and a fact. I think it is in reference to this distinction that it is necessary to define what we call the sense of sin.

The given which is here in question does not let itself be apprehended outside of a Love, more or less clearly conceived, the subject of which appears to himself like a work or object. Or at least where every clear notion of this Love is wanting there is in spite of everything a certain positing of oneself as soul, a certain relation to oneself which is of the essence of piety. Where all piety toward oneself is wanting there can no longer be anything which resembles the sense of sin. Moreover, this piety is very difficult to define. But it seems to me that it implies the affirmation of a transcendence. "We are not of here" said an old woman to J. with regard to the death of E." This is a naive but authentic way of affirming this transcendence. In as much as I consider myself as a simple fragment of nature, I place myself outside the condition of experiencing this sentiment of piety. However, in proclaiming that I do not belong to this world do I not thereby discredit this life here below? Is not the consciousness of sin confused with this condemnation of the natural life? It is certainly necessary to recognize that there exists here a possibility, a temptation; but I think there exists only a deviation there, which is, moreover, difficult to avoid. Whence this deviation? What would be the correct attitude? That is what I still do not see too well.

Le Peuch, March 6

What I retain from my remarks of yesterday is only the idea of a transcendence concealed in the feeling of sin. But transcendence over whom or what? This transcendence can be above all the quality of not belonging to myself. In a strictly monadistic ethic, assuming that such an ethic is possible, I do not see that there could be room for sin: for error yes. But it is here that the difference appears.

Le Peuch, March 7

I must also begin to take some notes for the metaphysical essay that Grenier has requested of me. I intend to use my notes of April, 1939.

The problem of reality starting with the affirmation. How is the affirmation possible? Is there any sense in contesting the right that I concede to myself of making affirmations? Affirmation as situated in relation to life.

I would like, on the other hand, to take a stand in reference to liberty and immortality. None of this is still clear in my mind. As always I have the disconcerting impression that I must start all over again from the beginning.

Le Peuch, March 8

As hazardous as it may be to affirm anything where it is a question of the most secret life of men, it does not seem rash to think that during the latter years the sense of sin has been weakened to the point of all but disappearing completely from consciences which have nevertheless not ceased to consider themselves Christian. Certainly there is no one who, in some determinate circumstances, may not be susceptible of undergoing the shock that accompanies this simple statement: "I have sinned," notwithstanding that he later treats this sentiment as a relic or a distant and deceitful echo of discarded beliefs. Actually it is much less a question of momentary states than of a permanent disposition that constitutes the continuous basis of the interior life. Still the word "disposition" is misleading in this context. We are dealing with this affirmation, sometimes vague and sometimes clear, "I am a sinner," or again and more profoundly, "We are all sinners."

One will not be astonished if one becomes aware of the indictments against Christian perspectives and morals which flourished since the disaster [of the war], amid the most suspect conditions, and which nevertheless in a general way were inspired by a vigorous and strong humanism. If so, one will not be surprised to find in them the old Nietzschean argument worn a little threadbare concerning the weakening action which the belief in sin exercises on consciences that are in process of being formed. At first we shall be quite legitimately tempted to give the simple answer that, especially in our country, the elements which have been found to be the least resistant have most often been those which were most seriously affected not only by laicism, but also by the chronic affections which the taste and the abuse of the power [to sin] cause, in the long run, in the depths of some souls. This display would not, however, suffice. Actually it would be very little in keeping with the demands of Christianity, taken in its fullness and such as it ought to be affirmed even at the level of reflection, to make Christians in general benefit from this massive exoneration. It seems infinitely preferable to interrogate oneself in all sincerity on the deviations and aberrations which the sense of sin can give rise to when it is not rectified by a dogmatic thought which is at once robust and comprehensive.

A general remark seems necessary here. The more the feeling in me of my own sin tends to reduce itself to the fear of not being according to the rate and as required by duty, and consequently of being found at fault in the final accounting for human actions, the more I am in danger of locking myself up in a system of obsessions of which I would remain the center, a system gravitating around the more or less precise image of my personal salvation or damnation. But to the degree that I will thus remain prisoner of self-centered conception of the personal drama and of the spiritual life, I may ask if, by the same token, I do not tend to place myself outside of Christianity understood in its eternal truth.

It is necessary to add that, at the same time, I will almost inevitably be led to transpose onto the moral as well as the religious plane the ways of being. These include the ways of feeling, as well as those of thinking and acting of the one who resorts to the utmost precautions for bringing to a successful conclusion an affair that is particularly dear to his heart. This is on the supposition that the preoccupation with salvation be real and not just a veneer on an existence which is not really involved in it and which continues to run its course according to its own laws.

We certainly will not contest the possibility that there may have been any number of people who subscribe, in all naiveté, to an individualism which has such deep roots in our condition as finite being. Moreover, we could hardly doubt that actually at a certain stage of the development of mankind, a conception of this order was needed in order to extricate man, I do not say from his egoism, but from the blindness which kept him from seeing ends that transcend by far the horizon of his immediate preoccupations.

In so far as we can without presumption hope to catch a glimpse, in its general outline, of the divine pedagogy which is at work in the history of human wisdom, it seems that the idea of individual salvation, considered in its most diverse expressions, has had to play an essential role. It is no less true that, when we consider it in a certain interior light, this notion is seen to be not only insufficient but little compatible with what is most original and most pure in the Christian aspiration properly so called. It stands to reason of course that between the representation of sin and that of salvation there exists here the most rigorous correspondence. In the terminology which I have so often used, it is not in the language of *having* that these fundamental notions can be truly expressed. By that I mean that we probably falsify the relations which are here implied when we declare that each of us will acquire merits destined to compensate, nay to *outweigh*, a certain initial taint. Whatever their ambiguity may be, their dangerous but fertile ambiguity, it is the ideas of life and death which must direct thought here. Each of us is a sinner to the extent that he happens to participate in a work of death which is accomplished in the world and with which we are associated, perhaps as much by our listlessness and our blindness as by this or that concrete and positively evil action.

Le Peuch, March 12, 1943

I have just re-read my notes of March, 1942. I do not think I have written anything more important. But I have not been able to turn to sufficient account my notes on life as a course.

Either we immobilize the other, the dead one, as though he had remained at some point of the course, or we imagine that this course runs parallel with ours, in a zone forbidden to our gaze. We must not absolutely exclude this second hypothesis. It does seem necessary, however, to succeed in bypassing this opposition between the stop and the course, and to conceive death as irreducible to one or other of these terms. We shall succeed all the less easily in doing so as we persist in relating it to ourselves. We shall succeed all the more as we are better able to restore it in its authenticity.

The only question that counts is to ascertain the conditions on which I can cease to be a prison for myself. It is in this way that the problem of salvation arises at the meeting point of the problem of being and the problem of freedom.

Le Peuch, March 13

The Sense and Consequence of Sin. The phrase "sense of sin" is certainly inadequate. "Sense" is here taken in the same way as when we speak of the moral sense or the sense of truth, an acceptation which does not involve anything affective. It is a question of a certain spontaneous power of acceptance or refusal. But in the case of sin there is yet another point. Not to have the sense of sin means to be incapable of apprehending oneself according to a certain spiritual dimension. In all probability natural reason is in effect incapable of it. Here arises the distinction on which I insisted, on the 4th or 5th of last March, between the feeling of imperfection and the feeling of sin. I can recognize my limitations, and can even suffer deeply from them without, by the same token, acknowledging that I am a sinner. As regards these limitations, I do not see that I am responsible for them. But beware! Does the feeling of sin merge with the feeling of responsibility? It seems almost certain to me that it is not. On the contrary, the more I put the stress on my responsibility, the more I risk showing myself a stranger to the feeling of sin. This is still not sufficiently clear.

This is what I mean: in the face of this or that failure, of this or that mishap of which others may have been victims as much as I and even more, I discover on reflection that it is I who have provoked this failure or this accident, for instance, because I neglected to take this or that precaution. This amounts to saying that I ought to have and that I could have [taken this precaution], and that I am therefore at fault. There is nothing here which is related to the consciousness of sin. Actually it seems that here again I can make a direct use of my retrospective observations exactly like an engineer who was first mistaken in his calculations but rectifies them later. If I am aware of my sin, that is of my condition as a sinner, I shall not labor under any illusions on this point. I will recognize that, left to myself, I shall not again "extricate myself from it"—at least not all alone—but that I will have to count on divine assistance in order to be spared from new setbacks. The consciousness of sin therefore opens out upon that of a necessary recourse. But here a twofold danger is possible. I could in some way take cover behind the idea of my sinful will in order to sink deep into a kind of fatalism ("After all, I cannot do anything about it!"). Or I can count exclusively on a will other than mine, that is, I no longer act, but let the other act, let things slide.

Such is, it seems to me, the twofold error that lies at the origin of the deviations so often denounced. One can claim in short that human life, considered in this perspective, becomes impoverished. We do not have the right to exploit to our advantage the fact of sin; that would amount to denying it; that would prove that we do not believe in it.

Whenever sin is misunderstood in its essence it can isolate us. On the other hand, it can bind us and become the principle of communion.

Le Peuch, March 14

These last remarks are essential. I do not have to derive any argument or pretext from the fact that my condition is that of a sinner in order not to make any effort. We could very simply say, and in keeping with the traditional good common sense, that I must on the contrary believe that the less I shall neglect myself, the more will the supernatural helps which I need be given to me. (It would be necessary to underscore the dangerous ambiguities that cling to the notion of self-neglect.)

There is here an equilibrium to be found; it can be realized only dynamically between what one might briefly describe as reason and faith. Surely, we have seen especially the abuses of a certain rationalism; but the latter, as a reaction, can give rise to a fideism which is hardly less dangerous.

It all clears up if we apply ourselves to consider sin from the angle of the *we* and not simply of the *I*.

Sin as milieu: living in sin. In this respect, an expression like "to commit a sin" is by its nature misleading. To commit a sin is to act as participating in this milieu in which we are all plunged. Let us, however, note that we can recognize its existence only to the degree that we emerge out of it. The Fall—independently of the more or less mythological accounts that have been given of it—can only be the event, in itself profoundly mysterious, through which a being created to the image of God has received darkness within him, and has himself partially become darkness. Consequently, it is necessary to be very prudent when we ask ourselves if this darkness would not have in some way pre-existed in the Fall. Who knows if we do not proceed here to a sort of retrospective objectification, or of extrapolation when we speak of pre-existence—and all the more so as it is perhaps meaningless to speaking of time before the Fall. Time is relative to the world—and perhaps there is a *world* only through and after the Fall.

I am far from hiding from myself the hazardous character of these last notes.

Le Peuch, March 15

The term "milieu" which I made use of yesterday is unsuitable. It is necessary to speak rather of "element." But the difficulty consists in understanding that this element is not a simple environment, that it penetrates me. Shall we make use of some medical notions and say that I constitute a favorable ground for the development of pathogenic germs which are widespread in this environment? Shall we say that something in me has as it were a natural affinity with this sin-element?

We must doubtless distrust very much this kind of comparison. However, if we are seeking to form a representation of sin, it is perhaps difficult not to appeal to notions of this order. But the obstacle and the danger are this: sin is in grave danger of being treated here in a natural way; in so far as it is Original Sin, it will be likened to the unfortunate predispositions which, for example, a tuberculous child manifests. From there it is only one step to recommending a prophylactic for sin, or a hygiene.

I think that there would be great interest in probing deeper into the notion of sin by beginning, not with these ideas or images, but with the obligation we have of rejecting them. On the one hand it would be necessary to note that sin develops in and through our conscience; this is far from being an objective datum which we could direct our attacks against as with an organic malady. On the other hand, it is necessary to note that there is everything to lose, as I have already said, in misunderstanding the supra-personal character of sin. The error or the mistake to the extent that the latter is only a variation of error can be verified and acknowledged. It seems that it is of the essence of sin that it can only be *revealed*, that is to say, basically it manifests itself only in the light of grace. The reason is, doubtlessly, because it transcends the immediate awareness that we may have of it. It would follow from this, it seems, that the philosopher as such cannot affirm the existence of sin.

I was telling myself this afternoon that the world seems to be directed toward sin to the extent that it seems to present itself as the center of a "teleology in reverse," that is, of a finality directed toward destruction. (It is in this sense that we can speak of the work of death.) But this teleology in reverse still does not seem to be sin.

On the other hand, I wonder if revelation does not bear essentially upon my insertion into an infinite community, or again upon my dependence in relation to God, which amounts to the same, God being the place of infinite communion. From this point of view, a conscience which is turned in upon itself and perhaps desiring to be self-contained, would oppose itself to revelation.

Le Peuch, March 16

I would wish to elucidate and to work out today certain remarks hurriedly jotted down yesterday. Fundamentally we are here faced with a paradox which borders on scandal. On the one hand, where there is no consciousness of self, therefore no responsibility, we cannot speak of sin. On the other hand, in as much as it is an element, sin seems to extend infinitely beyond the consciousness of the self. It would be necessary to attain an understanding of how sin penetrates man's self-consciousness. But here we must mistrust the imagination which turns the consciousness into something material and represents it as a sort of porous container, which really has no meaning. For this reason, I ought to apply myself to the task of seeing what precise meaning we can give here to the verb "penetrate" or "impregnate."

I begin to see clearly enough the order to be followed.

1. Within the notion of sin, is there anything which threatens to emasculate human nature? We believe that to be so when we put the emphasis on prohibitions

coming from the outside, when we imagine that the doctrine of sin confines man within the premises of the boarding school. But in reality nothing can be more superficial than such a notion. Instead, we must start from the analogy between sin and death. To believe in sin is to recognize that we are infinitely more affected than we think when we concentrate our gaze exclusively on the visible man.

2. Is any deviation of the idea of sin possible?

(a) An error which consists in devitalizing to excess both sin and salvation; a monstrous transposition, in this realm, of "each one for himself." (In all this, I am surely very strongly impressed by the views of Father de Lubac.)

(b) An error no less grave and which consists in forming for oneself a notion of salvation which is at bottom completely negative: above all, eliminate the risks—the ethic of safety. But no one can deny that this may be a caricatural deformation of the true Catholic doctrine.

All this is after all quite obvious and does not teach us very much. I must probe deeper by making use of my remarks of this morning, and resume the question which I formulated. At the bottom it is less a question of "penetration" than of "perversion." I take this word in its etymological sense: the fact of turning to the bad side. Must we say that conscience is perverted in so far as it turns to itself? I do not think so. Nevertheless, we would have to ask if the examination of conscience is not legitimate only when conscience orders an action upon itself. Perhaps, as contradictory as that seems, can we and must we act only upon ourselves, whereas we have to love only the other? The action upon the other, or the claim of acting upon the other, would be linked to self-love, for at bottom to act upon the other is to want to dominate him. It is not a question of denying that action upon the other is possible, but wherever it is direct and willed, perhaps it always partakes in some degree of violation.

Le Peuch, March 24

Perhaps I should put as an epigraph on my study: "At the same time and in unity of heart may we seek our souls and God" (Saint Augustine, *Soliloquies*, quoted by Father de Lubac).

Certitude. Its relation to existence and to value. Transition to involvement and sacrifice.

It seems that we must take as center the metaphysical certitude and the relation of this certitude to personal involvement.

Le Peuch, March 25

Take empirical certitude as my point of departure. The immediate as such is not the object of certitude. It is that only secondarily where it has been put in question by another. But can we not say, in a very general way, that there is place for certitude only where the other (would that be within me?) has first intervened? No certitude without an interpersonal reference since the other person can be reduced to an ideal schema.

On what grounds shall I proceed to a critique of the notion of certitude? An important question the terms of which it is necessary to define (this critique can be considered as a basis for all metaphysics).

Reflect on the plausible: why is the category of the plausible alien to metaphysics?

The indubitable. What is a concrete indubitable?

Distinction between what I actually doubt and what reflection shows me someone could doubt.

Le Peuch, March 26

Analyze the need of an indubitable in me, or rather for me. On what condition is this need legitimate? Investigate first the meaning of this question: What does legitimate mean here?

Are we dealing with a kind of portable certitude which I could hope to have at my disposal whenever I would want it and which *by the same token* may be within reach of everyone? Is it a question of discovering a minimum implication of experience, of every experience, to which every person will be bound to subscribe under pain of denying this experience itself? But supposing that this indubitable can be recognized, it will change nothing for me or for anyone. Now, what matters to me is a certitude which has a promotive, nay a creative value. An indubitable for anyone at all can be of no use to me; but an indubitable for anyone at all is, *in virtue of the connection between me and the other*, an indubitable for me at any moment, in any disposition. But what can count for me is rather something which I am not able to doubt when I am at a certain level of my self.

Let us say again:

a) that there would not be any interest in finding something which no one is able to doubt without absurdity;

b) but on the other hand—and this is one step further—I who do not doubt must not only take a stand in relation to the one who still doubts, but also find a means for making room for this doubt within the spiritual economy that I aim at promoting.[1]

All this amounts to saying that we have here an infinitely more complicated situation than one is wont to admit and to which it is necessary to be reconciled. However, one will object that the *savant* is in quest of a certitude which cannot reasonably be questioned. Here we would have to bring in the notion of an existential indubitable as opposed to an objective indubitable. This path leads to Kierkegaard. But we must find out how far we ought to go along this way.

I go back: reference to an interior conversation implied in certitude. Certitude shuts off; it puts an end to the discussion like the will. What conclusion is there to be drawn from this analogy?

Certitude has as its essence to declare itself, to proclaim itself. I do not see that it can in any way be detached from the declaration. But one declares, one proclaims only to. . . . It is necessary to add that it tends to form a deposit, as a result of this, from being an *act* it becomes a *having*. Whence an essential ambiguity. Can I take stock of my certitudes? That would be like a list of titles or possessions.

I must look for a point of departure. In conformity with the method which I have always followed, that point can be only the taking up the guidelines of a certain intuition which is mine and from which I cannot withdraw without disavowing myself or misrepresenting myself.

I must distinguish a certitude which bears on . . .

[1] I copy here a note jotted down yesterday evening in another notebook: "The only God in whom I can believe is a God who accepts, in a certain sense *who wills*, that it is possible to doubt Him." And this suffices to set aside all Spinozist or Hegelian philosophy. A concrete indubitable ought to have, as it were, assimilated the doubt without expressing it.

and a certitude which would be *being* and which would itself be a concrete indubitable; but because it is concrete, this indubitable is subject to eclipses. The notion of an eclipse, like that of the interior conversation, ought to take the top place in the study which I have in mind. Certitude in the second sense is subject to eclipse precisely because it is not possessed. This, however, is to be examined closely; for what is possessed can be lost, and if it could not, it would be meaningless. There are some complications here.

My situation is such that "some things" have happened to me. Still others will happen which probably depend on the first, but which in part, undoubtedly, have their roots elsewhere. These "things"—I employ this vague word with regret—appear to me, some as promoting, others as hindering a personal vocation which forms an integral part of me, even though I may not always be able to form a clear notion of it, that is, to define it for myself or for anyone else. I must note here, I think, that this vocation may or may not present itself as distinct from the reflection to which I proceed; but it does not seem that it can vanish entirely from me. Perhaps the term "gestation" would be preferable to that of vocation.

Le Peuch, March 27

I must take as my point of departure the opposition between going *toward* and going *adrift*. At every moment of my life, it is equally true, or unequally true, to say that I am oriented or engaged and that I am drifting. From the first point of view, there is a regulation more or less undergone, more or less assumed. Perhaps for the ambiguous term "vocation" I could better substitute "regulation" and "ordination." My organic life itself cannot be preserved without a minimum of regulation. My professional life, or even my family or sexual life can be only a completion or prolongation of it. My existence can thus appear to me, under all these aspects, as regulated. Nevertheless, when I consider this regulated existence, it may happen that it looks to me as if I am drifting. It will not be so if I am aware of an ordination. It is this notion that I must dig into. But I would first like to be assured that this research is useful for my work on metaphysical certitude.

Questions:
a) What did I think I was looking for?
b) What was I looking for in fact?
c) What would it be to have found?

a) That means: How have I represented the object of my research to myself?

b) This extensive conception of adherents or disciples has little by little been effaced at the same time, doubtless, that the awareness of a necessary philosophic polyphony was strengthened in me. For it is not true that one system integrates the others. It is necessary that each accepts the persistence of irreducibles.

In these conditions, can I say that I have really sought to satisfy myself? Doubtless, but that is after all only a tautology. Every research is directed toward a satisfaction, but the important point is to know what is the nature of this satisfaction. It is necessary to add that in any case I will not be able to satisfy myself if I am not aware at the same time and fundamentally, of satisfying the other, that is to say, of *giving*. To seek can only be to seek in order to give. But to give what? It is here that we just resume the notion of certitude.

It seems that I first seek to give myself this certitude and that I will tend, at the same time, to communicate it to the other. In a certain sense, I have to treat myself as a neophyte, or to be initiated. Under one of its aspects, my research is initiation. However, where is the initiator?

Le Peuch, March 29

I believe there is nothing to be retained from these last remarks. It is a dead end.

Le Peuch, March 30

In this kind of exposition in which I have been invited to participate (the collective volume on Existence, to be published by Gallimard), what do I have to "produce"? Would not the ideal be to have all prepared, fully formulated, some metaphysical theorem accompanied by its demonstration and which would pass on to posterity with my name? To be sure, in such a domain, we cannot hope to reach the incontestable. But would it not be something satisfying to provoke at least one of those discussions which have always delighted the heart of professors? Why would I seek to conceal from myself that I previously conceived the function of the philosopher in this way? But also, the sharper my reflection became, the more has this way of conceiving this function become strange to me. Thus to the question: "What have you to produce or to show?" I would be tempted to reply: "Nothing really." I would even be tempted to go on to the counterattack and to declare very clearly that if one claims to discern what constitutes the reality of a philosophic thought, it is never on the plane of the exposable, that is, of the textbook, that it must be placed. As conscientious as a textbook of the history of philosophy may be, it never presents to us any but the most absurd spectacle of the "massacring game." It is in this game that the deepest part of me refuses to participate. But in so doing do I not deliberately put myself outside the game? Is it really only a question of a game? Is it in this way that I can qualify the kind of gestation which, for thirty-five years, was going on within me? Surely not. But what sort of gestation? Doomed to what kind of miscarriage? Really, it is easy to imagine this miscarriage; but if perchance the expected childbirth takes place, what is it that is given birth to?

Le Peuch, March 31

That still gives me the impression of a false start. I must confine myself to the notes on the two indubitables.

Last evening I was thinking to myself that the idea of a *system valid for all* had still to be deepened. Each one is basically treated as a pure reader, that is to say, as participating in a certain game. It is within the enclosure reserved for this exercise that everything happens and is decided; hence the deplorable, the artificial impression that so many philosophical controversies give. The reader is as it were withdrawn from the tragedy of existence. He is someone for whom the vital problems are no longer posed or, more precisely, for whom the drama of existence is, at least momentarily, suspended. It subsists bracketed. Impurity is due to the fact that this system procures notoriety or consecration to the one who has invented it. Of course, one does not labor under an illusion; one does not claim to refute all the objections, but one hopes that in principle they will at least be reduced.

But through a healthy dialectic, that philosophy has

no sooner become official than it reveals its insufficiencies, and by the same token the intrinsic absurdity which is the secret defect of all official philosophy appears in full light. Reasons why the most anti-official philosophy inevitably tends to become official, against the express wish of those who first conceived it.

The existential indubitable as indubitable, not only for me, but *for us*, that is, for those who communicate with me, which is possible only at a certain level of experience, of our experience. Tendency to gradual diffusion, but this has nothing comparable to the mechanical propagation of which the textbook is the vehicle. Return to Socratism.

Le Peuch, April 1

Tonight I thought that I would make the exigence of immortality the pivot of my study:

—the category of the ludicrous,

—death as image [*simalacre*]

—the idea of an ontological counter-balance for death,

—the "we" as constellation.

This investigation could be linked with my reflections on the existential indubitable. Indeed, immortality does not have to be proved as an objective fact. Although something inclines us invincibly and despite all to aspire to this demonstration, at the same time, we are capable of transcending this aspiration: I always come back to the last scene of *The Iconoclast*, which remains one of the pivots of my work.

It seems that I will manage to discern the articulations of such an investigation. It is in relation to the loved one that we can understand how, by treating death as an ultimate given, we are invincibly led to proclaim the ludicrous character of life. I must define the meaning of these two words.

The ontological counter-balance of death is the presence in me of those who have a part in me, who have made me what I am and continue to make me. The veneration of the dead necessarily implies without doubt an analogous presence. When we speak here of remembering, it is the lack of metaphysical equipment which would permit giving an account of the experience which we want, not only to translate, but to consecrate.

Le Peuch, April 3

I do not know what to think of the preceding notes. I have the impression that they are very vague.

Le Peuch, April 7

A possible new point of departure (following the letter which I wrote yesterday to Louis A. on the subject of the sometimes obstructive role played by the *detail* in life). It would be called: "From everyday [life] to metaphysics," or rather: "The metaphysical tenor of human experience." It will be necessary to call attention immediately to the fact that it is on purpose that I have taken this Heideggerian title in order to indicate the relation between us; the irreducible differences will stand out subsequently. The phenomenological description of everyday life presented by Heidegger has a tendentious quality; it seems that it cannot be accepted as such.

To begin with two rejoinders from "Hungry Hearts": "On what do you live?—I am like the others, I live only on the condition of not asking myself that question."

On what do you live? What are your resources? What does this word "resources" mean here? The question also means: Who procures for you these indispensable resources? Do you not live as if you possessed resources which are really lacking in you? But if you live on credit, who then extends you the credit? Before whom do you risk finding yourself insolvent one day?

All these questions arise only if we admit that life—in a sense which itself remains to be defined—requires an effort which is perpetually beginning again. What is "that which permits me" to make this effort? But a confusion is here possible. My organic life needs to be nourished, I cannot maintain it except on condition that I eat, sleep, etc. Does this I answer the question raised? No. On the one hand, it can happen that, although I am fed, I do not find within me the courage to continue living. On the other hand, we can also say that these organic functions cannot be exercised without my consent: I can let myself die.

Here again, what is lacking is a certain basic courage. The meaning of the word courage is very close to that of the word "heart": "I do not have the heart to . . ." From here on, the problem of resources consists in asking what gives me the courage to. . . . One would surely be tempted to appeal to the idea of a certain vitality which is deployed within every reflection, or even every thought: I can state that I continue to eat, to sleep, but I do not really know why; the machine goes on functioning, but it is as though I disowned it: we are as it were dissociated, it and I. An insupportable duality: "This is no longer life!" My existence as it were has degenerated. Without exaggeration I could say that *I no longer live*; this is the expression which comes to the lips when one is in the last degree of anguish: "I am no longer living since Pierre is in the war." . . .

Passage to the notion of *ennui*. *Ennui* taken in the strong sense, consequently cannot be used in the plural. To pine away.

In the deserted Orient, how my ennui grows! (Bérénice). When I pine away, I no longer live:

One single being is missing to you, and the whole world is disenchanted.

Why? Because you yourself have been hurt to the point of losing all possibility of animating the world in which you are thrown. However, we should not interpret in a purely subjectivistic sense this power of animation of which you find yourself at present deprived. And I might add that the power to grasp is before all a power to lend oneself, that is to say to let oneself grasp (role of the *kairoi*). Hardening. Locking, which results in my not being able to lend myself. It is because I no longer dispose of myself that I am no longer able to be at the disposal of others.

It would now be necessary to find out what is the relation between all that and value: to recapture the notion of value as appeal, to which purpose I dedicated my letter yesterday to Louis A. . . . . To be no longer interested in anything: "Since I lost M. I can no longer be interested in anything." Oscillation between emptiness, a sorrowful emptiness, and obsession. The value here disappears, for what is concentrated in the obsessing image is not value. This means that I am deaf to every appeal; I no longer exist. But this negative way of expressing such a situation is really improper. The everyday subsists, but in a unique way like a chain impossible to shake off. There are burdens, obligations from which I cannot be freed, and I do not myself even know exactly why.

How value can be reintroduced: analogy with air or light. All is not dead.

The everyday degraded. The everyday consecrated and regenerated.

The day: real unity between two real nights. The day: link in an abstract chain treated as homogenous; it is in terms of this notion that the everyday is degraded (gloomy perspective, play of mirrors).

Le Peuch, April 8

The de-ontological point of view of the everyday. The everyday as the basis of regulation (one must say one's prayer each day, but also one must brush one's teeth, etc.). But it is precisely against this regulation that I am tempted to revolt. Uniformity. The everyday experienced as prison. Attempt at evasion: I will no longer wash, I will no longer shave, I will no longer actively participate in this universal routine which irritates me. I will not go out either, for I do not want to be exposed to meeting the same people in the same places everyday. I shall thus avoid the outrage which the everyday reality inflicts upon me, I who am not of here, but whose true fatherland is elsewhere!—But how can I help not seeing that in this way I plunge into the non-existent, I do not draw near to this fatherland which is far away and which for me is only a state of nostalgic yearning. I sink below the everyday, that is to say, into the infra-human. In order to transcend the everyday, would I not have to appeal to the unlimited resources of abstraction?

Here it is necessary to introduce a definition of the metaphysical: the metaphysical is not the meta-empirical, that which transcends all possible experience. Can we say, or must we say, that a metaphysical experience exists? But the expression is ambiguous. Can we say that there are objects which would be accessible to a certain kind of experience? Or rather would it not be necessary to say that it is not through the object that the experience is here specified? Is it, then, through a certain subjective quality? No. Rather it would be by a certain mode of tension within that which, when analyzed, is arbitrarily separated into subjective and objective. Could we not say, in this sense, that all experience involves an extremely variable content of what we call, rather improperly, the metaphysical tenor? I must find some examples to illustrate what I mean. A sensible experience could here be used, but will it be necessary to say that it is used in so far as it presents itself as illustrating symbolically a certain idea? Certainly not. Rather in that it awakens in us a certain repercussion.

Le Peuch, April 9

Metaphysics is not the domain of entities, it is the very opposite of that. We must understand, however, by what fatal error it is sometimes reduced to that.

This *metaphysical tenor of experience*—it is precisely by starting from the everyday that we can see in what it consists. The everyday, pure and simple, disregards the metaphysical: The everyday as devaluated or depreciated denies it; the everyday as consecrated or regenerated affirms it. Is that a faulty way of expressing the matter? No, for the everyday is experience, and every human experience as such expresses itself and becomes language. We might say that what is within language is in a certain sense even within the experience.[1]

The everyday pure and simple is the experience of

---

[1] Let us say more precisely that experience does not become experience except to the extent that it is formulated, for it is only on this condition that it communicates with itself and becomes thereby transmissible.

the one who, at every moment, is "at his business":
sufficient for the day is the evil thereof. It would be
inaccurate to say that it is life in the instantaneous. The
everyday manifests itself as a succession of tasks to be
accomplished, each of which has a certain duration.
This succession does not exclude a certain overlapping
of tasks in their relation to one another (for example,
in the life of a housewife who sweeps the room while
the soup is cooking in the pot, etc.). The more the
everyday is split up into well-defined tasks which are
linked one to the other, the more does the metaphysical
tenor of human experience seem to be reduced. However, we feel that the truth of the matter is not purely
and simply thus; do we not have to distinguish the
spirit in which these tasks are carried out? But what do
we understand by this "spirit"? Is it not an entirely
subjective disposition, a sort of coloring? And we would
be led to think in principle that, if there is a metaphysical element at the heart of human experience, it must
be immanent in the latter's structure or in its composition. But we should greatly mistrust these metaphors,
all of which are misleading.

Experience is not comparable to a ready-made object
that is subsequently covered with a dressing. Nothing is
more important than recognizing how difficult it is to
think of experience. We cannot refrain from imagining
it with the aid of metaphors borrowed from it, but
which, by definition, it overflows on all sides. It is thus
that, when we speak of its metaphysical tenor, we imagine it as retaining some fragment of a certain unaltera-
ble substance to which we have access only indirectly or
secretly by some roundabout way, or also as reserved for
a limited class of the privileged or the initiate. But it is
clear that we have to free ourselves from these material-
izing images. Experience is not a bath; metaphysical

reality is not a body. Here it would be necessary to ask ourselves what leads us to raise the question. It is evidently because we note differences in level, let us say more precisely of saturation, among our experiences (but here again language crystallizes into material imagery).

Here the notion of value will come up: the memorable is what it is because it has a meaning, a value. Difference to be noted: a breakfast can be worth remembering; it can be this, quite surely, on the gastronomical level. It can also be this, despite the ordinariness of the food, because of a certain quality of the atmosphere. Here we have two systems of values. Is it enough to say that these are different systems without there being any hierarchy between them? But we have to recognize that a personal life implies a hierarchy and is personal only on this condition.

Perhaps we must here introduce the notion of the extraordinary. To investigate the relations between order and the extraordinary. The degenerated everyday seems to exclude the extraordinary; it is in breaking loose from the everyday that we seek to join the extraordinary. But there can also be an extraordinary that is immanent in order itself. What does extraordinary mean here? It is not a matter of departing from the legal order which by itself is boring and deceptive.

The changeable power of irradiation immanent in personal experience. Art is not intelligible otherwise and that is what makes art "the eternal document of metaphysics" (Schelling). A being has value in the precise measure in which, through his example and his work, he will have developed and renewed our reasons for loving. But this power can be turned against being, against love.

Conques, April 12

Yesterday, I jotted down a few words in my blue notebook on the characteristic which privation has for sharpening the memory of what we have to do without. But this does not seem to have any knowable relation with what I wrote at Peuch before leaving. It would, however, be necessary to ask about the role which privation plays in daily experience. The privation, I said, is always a certain being of non-being; pure and simple nonpossession is not a privation. I am deprived only of what I have had and which in some way still resides in me.

I must come to direct grips with the problem of the relations between me, or any person, and experience; a problem very difficult to state in intelligible terms, for we have nothing to gain in treating the person as the subject of experience.

Conques, April 13

To *conduct* an experiment. Where the experience is deliberate or premeditated, where it is comparable to a set of operations, the I is effectively the subject. But we must see that our life as a whole does not let itself be compared to an experiment conceived in this fashion. Can I not, with good reason, imagine that I am as it were the place in which is carried out an experiment of which I do not possess all the data and the ultimate meaning of which I do not know? (Whereas where I conduct an experiment, where I proceed to an experiment, I know where I am going, at least approximately.) But we must be very careful not to be hasty in imposing a name on the active force which is the true subject of this experiment of which I would be the place, in speaking for example of the genius of the species, of the *Zeitgeist* [spirit of the age], etc.

This morning I began to wonder if I would not have to take up again topics from further back still, that is to say, beginning with the very notions of being, of non-being, of becoming.

It would then be necessary to ask on what conditions the word "being" has a meaning for me. (For me: is this not subjectivism? No, for what can be communicated to myself is what can be communicated to the other.) We would have to carry out an analogous inquiry for the term "to have value" and to compare the results. Perhaps I should begin with that very important page from *Being and Having* on affirmation. "Wondering if I am," is this a contradiction in terms, since I cannot ask myself this question if I am not? But someone could reply: there is not necessarily a contradiction: is the one who asks this question the "I" whose being is put in question? Here the German language is infinitely more illuminating: *Es wird gefragt ob Ich bin* [it is asked whether I am]. Again we might say that the wholly ideal mode of existence which belongs to a condition as such is entirely different from the reality which is here pointed as problematic. We could distinguish between ideal being and substantial being. We should then admit a distinction of degree within being. But what is it that permits me to affirm the insufficiency of what I have called "ideal being"? Is it not necessary that a reference be made to a different being which would be, or would have been, experienced to begin with? But experienced by whom, if not by me?

I must next refute the position which consists in isolating the "I."

Being as the pledge or seed of eternity. And yet, could it not be only an instantaneous flash?

Exaltation in the unfolding of the self (the tree in blossom).

Noon. It seems to me that the note jotted down this morning can be put to use but on condition that the meaning and scope of the question raised are more clearly indicated. I must bring into relief the fact that here the question is not really separable from the exigency. I must begin with everyday experience: thus a connection is established with my notes at Peuch at the beginning of April.

I look at myself through my daily experience. I do not have the slightest reason to doubt the existence of the beings and things with which I have dealings; I am at the mercy of these beings, of these things. But these dealings tend to absorb me completely; I immerse myself in them. My body needs to be nourished, to be exercised, to be rested; my body which is in no way privileged with regard to other things. The everyday life manifests itself primarily by the cycle of organic functions; it is with regard to this recurrence that I have to take a stand. It can be presented to me in such a manner that I am violently tempted to cut it short; and the fact that I do not yield to this temptation can have no meaning or can be mere cowardice.

Conques, April 15

Basically, all this leads up to the conclusion that the problem of being or non-being has meaning only where it is transformed into the dilemma: plenitude or death. It arises from this ambiguous existence which is mine and which is carried out day after day through the round of functions and tasks. This is therefore a problem of evaluation. But here again we must ask ourselves if we are in the realm of the purely subjective. Phenomenologically it is certain that the value "being"—if it is truly a value—does not manifest itself to me as being conferred by me on something which of itself would not or could not include it. Here the term "plenitude" is instructive. But we could also utilize the distinction between the closed and the open, or again the notion of captivity to which I have appealed in connection with hope. I must ask what it means to be captive, or to appear to myself as captive to the round of functions and tasks. I must resume my previous notes on *disgust*. Link between *disgust* and *stench*; decomposition; captivity tends to undo me. There is here a meeting of thoughts which I have expressed here and there. Captivity is already death—death in the midst of life; but is that not pre-eminently death? We could say that death purely and simply is either nothing or is a chance for liberation. But perhaps, will it be only what we have made it; will not death after life be the death we have deserved according as we have succumbed to death within life or have on the contrary triumphed over it?

Provided we take the categories of life and death in a non-biological sense, we are right in substituting them for those of being and non-being. But this substitution, delicate and perilous, is indispensable.

I must do away with all solipsism, full or masked. There is no sense in saying that I know only my states of consciousness; to the extent that they are mine, I live them, I do not know them. If I convert them into objects, I liken them to external objects.

Thus, no ontological prerogative belonging to the privileged *who* that I would say is myself. I cannot even speak of absolute proximity, for I can sometimes feel myself closer to some other than to myself. The notion of proximity is itself interesting, it is really that which is in question. The idealist starts with the idea of an absolute proximity, but proximity to what? Evaluated by whom? It is important to ask how it can happen that I feel withdrawn from myself, alienated. My structure must permit this sentiment of alienation, and there is no sense in saying that this sentiment does not correspond to anything.

We must moreover dig deeper into the notion of prerogative: a prerogative can be, in principle, only given or conceded; here it would be necessary to say that the "I" gives a prerogative to itself. But this is not really the question that is at stake; instead, it is the matter of the claim that the "I" enjoys in respect to itself a privileged situation. The other would intervene only as an *eidōlon* in the magic circle that the "I" forms with itself. This, however, would suppose that the "I" is given to itself before every other reality, but this priority is illusory.

Le Peuch, April 16

It seems that all my notes of these last few days are beginning to get organized.

What does the distinction or opposition between being and non-being mean for me? Let us not be deceived by the subjectivistic appearance which the question presents. What is important is to know on what condition this opposition can be made living and thereby communicable for me. I do not deny that there may be for me an incommunicable and that the latter may be able as such to manifest a value; but that is not what I am here occupied with. Granted that I speak of the incommunicable, it will be with the intention of communicating something about this subject and con-

sequently of inciting the other to turn toward this
incommunicable which ought to be in him as in me. I
wonder for example on what condition I can attribute a
certain being to non-being or to a certain non-being.
For me it will be a matter of delving deep enough in
my experience, in order to see to what such an assertion
can refer. Is it not of the essence of my experience
sometimes to canonize itself, sometimes on the contrary to proclaim its own nothingness? It would be
necessary to ask, however, if in this case we are not the
dupes of words; how would it be within the power of
any experience to pronounce a judgment upon itself?
Must we not rather think that an experience is given to
a subject who appreciates it or eventually condemns it?
But I wonder if this way of conceiving things, still in
vogue, is not based on an illusion. What would this
subject be? Do we not have here a pure and simple
transposition, under a sketchy form, of the idea of a
judge who hears a case or pronounces a verdict? Someone will say: it is the opposite that is true; the judge in
question is essentially a function that is carried out. It
will be agreed that this function is not carried out in
the absolute, but one will discern there the mark of the
imperfection of the creature, incapable of being fully
identified with his function. Now, there can be a mistake here, for to judge is to judge in the concrete and
with all of oneself.

But I seem to be going astray, although these remarks have the advantage of bringing into relief any
element of the fallacious which the idea of a pure
subject, of a subject-function (Kant) can have.

I would like if possible to try now to set out the plan
of the projected study. I propose to call to mind some
essential metaphysical categories, without any explicit

reference to philosophical doctrines, even the most recent; to make every effort to discern what these categories mean and are worth for me.

The very notion of the metaphysical. It seems equally false:

(1) to conceive the metaphysical as the meta-empirical, as transcending every possible experience;

(2) to imagine that it can constitute a privileged sphere to which we would be given access by a special type of experience.

But from the fact that the metaphysical is not the reserved, must we conclude that it consists in short in the frame of an experience, of whatever sort it be? Before answering, it is necessary for us to ask what guides us in this discussion; it can only be the awareness of a certain exigence, the perception of a certain appeal to which it will be our endeavor to respond as exactly as possible. Metaphysical exigence brought close to the exigence of creation.

Aspiration to be initiated to a certain secret, less and less conceived, however, as equivalent to the possession of a power over things; and by the same token it appears that it is less and less with things that we are concerned. The case of things appears more and more hopeless.[1] We will never have more than mere access to increasingly more perfect techniques of which they are the locus. Considered on a plane outside of all possible technique they cease to be things. It is from this point of view—but from this point of view only—that we can ask ourselves if they are really outside of us. They come nearer to me according as I become aware of my own

---

[1] By that I mean we believe less and less in a secret of things, it seems to us, rightly or wrongly, that they do not have any "inside."

"strangeness"; they blend with me at the limit, at the point where I disappear from my own eyes.

Le Peuch, April 17

What is essential is this possible fluctuation of experience; it is in no way comparable to an opaque and constant datum, and it is for that reason that it is so difficult to conceive it. It is in terms of this variation that the metaphysical can and ought to be posited (a variation which goes on between the customary and the strange). The metaphysical is imagined as being on the outside of experience only where the latter is arbitrarily stabilized. On the other hand, the more experience appears unstable and diversified, the more is the metaphysical grasped as being immanent in it. Could we not be content, however, with a relativistic pluralism? That would mean that among the various modalities that experience can affect one could not set up a hierarchy based upon a principle that is independent of the individual's preferences. To the extent that, *by means of abstraction,* I consider things independently of myself, of their relation to me, this is probably the case. But it is just this abstraction which is untenable. It would be necessary to take an example: the experience of fields such as it presents itself to the peasant who cultivates them and to the poet who wrote the *Georgics.* I feel, however, that the question is badly put; I still have to work on it.

All that I have just written and which is not complete is perhaps only a parenthesis breaking the continuity of thought.

I come back to what I wrote at the end of my notes of yesterday and which had not been sufficiently explained. Things cannot be separated from the techniques which permit us to manipulate them; now this manipulation is itself conceivable only in a world of pure exteriority, a world of elements acting on one another. There is a way in which I can say there exists, not merely a similarity, but an identity of nature between my body and things; *my body is a thing*, and it is condemned to follow the destiny of things, particularly of instruments. Like them, it is useful, it needs to be maintained, sometimes even repaired. It ends up by being thrown away on the scrap heap. It is subjected to vicissitudes which are wholly comparable to those which tools undergo. It can also be compared to a work of art, to the extent that it is a source of enjoyment and, in this respect also, it is condemned: the work of art will not be able to sustain an unlimited number of restorations, etc.

All this is true, but not enough. Someone might say that this body belongs only to a subject who identifies himself with it while opposed himself to it. But away with abstractions. My body does not reveal itself as a tool which I could do without because I can find another for it, or because I can exercise some other activities for which I have no need of it. It is given to me as the absolute condition of all possible instrumentality —and also of all possible enjoyment; in this sense it is given to me as being my all, with this reserve, however, that it retains—or rather that I retain, by means of it—the possibility of sacrificing myself. Yes indeed, even here its mediation remains indispensable: it is my hand that presses the trigger of the revolver or which turns on the gas. This is enough to show that it remains a means—therefore that it is not the whole; because the whole would not be exclusively a means. Certainly, no one will dispute the point that this means tends to take itself as an end. Where material life is not rigorously controlled, it tends to become a closed system; but the fact that this control is possible suffices to show that the body is not all, that materialism is not true and even that it is absurd.

All that we can say is that it belongs to my condition that the absolute instrument through which I affirm myself, for others and perhaps for myself, can tend to behave as an entity subsisting not surely by itself but for itself. It is useless to point out that this is conceivable only by abstraction. My subsistence can be assured only by means of an extraordinarily complex group of mediations of a social nature, but it is conceivable that I may end by taking myself as the center of the whole social organism. In that case the others do not interest me except to the degree that they contribute to the satisfaction of my needs, whatever they be.

From this point of view, we directly and easily come to the notion of transcendence. Perhaps it is not fitting to speak here of a notion. It would be necessary to ask if this is not *the reality* of a transcendent which is implied in the fact of sacrifice or even of suicide. (I note today, January, 1959, that we are here close to Dostoievsky's Kirilov in *The Possessed*.)

The opposition to be established between sacrifice truth is that there seems to be no sense in opposing idea to reality. The reality of the transcendent consists in this that it is an idea and operates as an idea. For example, the reality of the fatherland can in no way be distinguished from the idea of fatherland which animates the patriot. Doubtless, the same holds good for the believer. Let us note here the role of interior eristic in the course of which the body finds a spokesman in a thought which represents it and which attacks the idea: "You are only an idea, it says for example to the fatherland, and as for me, I have behind me the only unquestionable reality." We must not however be the dupes of words. What is this thought delegated by the body? How would this delegation be conceivable? What are the real qualifications of this thought which claims to invalidate every affirmation bearing on the transcendent?

Le Peuch, April 18

This delegation is invented; it is the justification which a thought gives to itself while claiming, in the name of the real, to depreciate what is only ideal.

From what I wrote yesterday it follows that it is of the essence of my body that it can and must be considered in turn as "I" and as "not I." It is also in this perspective that one could consider abnegation.

Note, that from the time I sacrifice myself as body, I sacrifice my future: the body as the reserve of the future; to give my life is precisely to renounce this future. But on what condition is this sacrifice possible? It supposes a disengagement; it is from the rut of everyday life that I have to disengage myself. What are we to understand by that if not that I have dug out for myself what I could regard indifferently as either a shelter or a prison. We find here again the round of functions and tasks which I referred to during these latter days. I am in this life in the very sense that I am in my body, for it is surely altogether arbitrary to reduce the body to the form it displays at a given instant. The body is a certain way of enduring. From this point of view, to be disembodied is not essentially to be transported or to appear *elsewhere*; it is to escape this mode of enduring which has become natural to me, which occurs in ecstasy. It may happen that my life does not, in my own eyes, reveal me and even that it horrifies me

(Cf. Christiane in Act IV of *The Broken World*). What does this mean? Must we say that this is a pure illusion?

Le Peuch, April 19

All this seems to me rather confused. I do not cease to continue living because my life displeases me. All that I can say is that I am unhappy about it, that I feel badly about it; but this is surely not enough for me to free myself of it. On the contrary, it can be thought that there is a way of protesting against it which has the effect of closing it on me. We might even wonder if accepting life is not the preliminary condition which is imposed on the one who intends to free himself of it. Only, the meaning of this word is not altogether clear.

I do not have the feeling that the notes of these past days can be turned to account.

Le Peuch, April 22

I aspire to certitude. We shall have to ask what that means. I long to be in a situation such that I can pronounce myself to be certain. But is it that I aspire to any certitude whatever, be it even that which would consist in the recognition that life, the world, does not have any meaning? Would the fact of having to establish myself in this certitude put an end to my anguish? Far from it, it would perpetuate it. This negative certitude would entail only one advantage: it would permit me to triumph over those who persist in believing in an intelligible or providential order; it would satisfy what turns out to be a pretension in me, the will to affirm myself against the other, to dominate. Also pride in not being taken in, in knowing that one has not been tricked.

It is important to ask if, in aspiring to a certitude, it is essentially the satisfaction of this pride which is sought. I must note in passing, perhaps, the contradiction that lies in this, that, in a world which would be mere nothingness, a judgment can be passed by which the world would be condemned. After all, I who declare the nothingness universal claim to exist; and if, on reflection, I myself am included in this condemnation, either I do not know what I am saying, or I am in the abyss, the non-thought. Consequently I renounce my certitude.

There is a sense in which it is surely true to say that the mode of existence which is mine consists primarily of *being in quest* of a certitude: comparison with a body which moves itself so long as it has not attained equilibrium.

To be certain of. . . . I must reflect more deeply on the meaning of these words. There lies an abyss. . . . Is certitude the entirely negative experience of the fact that I do not have any doubt? But this is an illusion. Why do I not have any doubt? This negation itself rests on something positive. On what? On the fact that something *has revealed itself* to me (in the way in which love reveals itself).

Le Peuch, April 26

In the letter which I wrote to Louis D. I pointed out that there is no meaning in passing a judgment of intrinsic value or non-value upon everyday life as such. In as much as the everyday life does not exist, it can either depersonalize and thereby degrade itself, or on the contrary it can regenerate itself through a spirit of love which magnetizes it. Of what is it made, this everyday life? Or rather, in what does it consist? In functions and tasks: my days are spent in. . . . I also note that despair seizes me as soon as I have the feeling that my days fall one after the other, like homogenous units, into the depth of an abyss and that I have no more than an unknown but limited number of them left to spend up to the moment when I shall have no more left: I shall be at my tether's end. Thereby I am comparable to the one who squanders his capital. It is not so to the extent that I accomplish a work, no matter what it be. And yet, in the presence of an accomplished work, I can feel indifferent and almost hostile, just as in the face of my posterity. It can happen that this work seems to me to be so detached from me that what will happen to it no longer interests me. I shall then go to the length of maintaining that it was owing to an optical illusion that I was concerned about it and about what would become of it.

This separate "I" seems to affirm itself as mortal precisely by the way in which it separates itself from what is not it. The perpetuation of naked existence to which it aspires is not conceivable without a contradiction. Someone may perhaps retort: what I aspire to is not simply to continue to exist, but to continue to participate, for example in the life of my family or of my country; it is to remain associated with. . . . I do not see that this wish has anything of the absurd or impious, but it seems that it cannot be realized unless this association takes place according to new modalities which I can represent to myself only imperfectly, for it may very well be that they are irreducible to *having an awareness of* . . .

Le Peuch, April 28

The property of the existent is to be involved or inserted, that is, to be in a situation or in communication. Consequently, if, when claiming to posit it, one abstracts not only from such a situation but from every situation whatever, one substitutes for it, if not a pure fiction, at least an idea.

There is no point in contesting the existence of the external world, let us say, things, if at the same time my own existence is not denied to me who not only perceives them but is in communication with them. But can I contest my existence? What do I have in mind when I contest it?

Le Peuch, April 30

The channel starting from the presence of the other to myself: it is mysterious. But the reason is that one opposes this presence as a problematic idea to the fact of the presence of oneself to oneself considered as a solid given, as an invariant. Now it is precisely this postulate that ought to be challenged. Presence to oneself is not an invariant. One forms an intellectual notion of it and thereby one misunderstands its essence. I am not at all present to myself in an invariable way. On the contrary I am most often alienated or decentered. And when, from the depth of this alienation, I try to grasp what presence to myself is, I can no longer imagine it, no longer believe in it. But as much as I cease to "realize" what my own presence to myself can be, I all the more make myself unable to believe in the other's presence to myself. In reality everything becomes clear from the moment one understands that presence to oneself is blended with creativity. Still we must immediately point out that creativity does not mean productivity; to create is not to produce.

There is an obscurity here: in what sense am I justified in saying that it is I who am present to myself? Would it not be better to speak of [the presence of] being or of reality? It is indeed necessary to observe that the "I" can designate only an absence, more precisely only a lack—and at the same time that this lack is almost invariably disposed to treat itself as being something positive. The illusion of the "I" is nothing else. But this only helps to reinforce the doubt. Do we not, with Lavelle, come to place the presence of being at the root of self-consciousness? It is here, I think, that we must appeal to a phenomenology of everyday experience. But this is still not precise enough.

Perhaps I should set out with the idea of our relation with the other, and preferably with the absent other, the missing other in order to criticize it. This is the point of departure for my note of this morning. That is where I seemed to have had a sort of light before I got up.

I recall at this moment Emile M., who was killed in May, 1940. I might be told: "He cannot be present to you; all you have is a small film reduced to its simplest expression. You can turn this film or this record, that is all. However, there is no sense in saying that this film or this record is him." However, a protest against this reduction rises up from the depth of my being. A protest stemming from love; a protest which is love itself. An affirmation which bears on ipseity linked to the critique of the idea of likeness. I shall say: "Nothing of what has been human can lapse into the state of a simple likeness, or, which amounts to the same thing, can disappear by simply deputatizing for itself a devitalized imitation of itself. I must investigate the nature of this affirmation: it is a challenge. This affirmation is by no means a statement of fact; it is quite the opposite, like hope. The characteristic of a statement of fact is that it can be verified, which in this case is unthinkable.

But this does not make the essential point clear and one cannot at any rate be content with saying that presence is mystery. What do I mean when I say, "It is not merely the image of Emile M. that I carry within me, it is he himself"? The image is only a means by which a reality continues to be communicated to me; an act of transcendence which is at the root of invocation and of worship. But we must try and clarify this by starting with the presence to oneself. It seems possible to make use of the experience of reassessment in the opposite way. I again become present to myself only within the experience of a certain renewal and by means of a preliminary sleep. However, the question remains: By what right can I say that I am present to myself? Consciousness of a freedom. But there is nothing to guarantee that this freedom is not at bottom a grace. There is something there that is only given or *granted* to me, and the conditions for which neither can be enumerated nor are they capable of being reproduced at will.

To say that I am in quest of a certitude seems to express correctly the mode of existence that is mine in as much as I am, not just a living being, nor a citizen or dramatic author, but a philosopher. On reflection this formula reveals itself as still ambiguous. The characteristic of certitude is to declare itself; it does not seem that it can really be dissociated from the act by which it is communicated. But then, to say that I am in quest of a certitude, is it not to say simply that I am looking for words to express a certain state, a certain experience which was perhaps already mine before I undertook this research? Or else, is this to say—which would be quite another matter—that I am in quest of a way of being which lends itself to the mode of formulation by which a certitude is expressed? A way of being or a way of knowing? If it is a question of my gaining access to a new type of knowledge, it will by the same token be a question of finding myself put in a new relation with regard to what I have to know. This change of position bears essentially on the manner of being.

The alternative thus presented seems really very simple. It is unfortunately doubtful that the reality within which my effort develops lends itself to such an elementary kind of option. By supposing even a fundamental invariance in the original experience which is mine, we shall have to recognize that, in order to make room for the formulas which I set myself to discover, it must be organized, it must materialize. It is necessary for that matter that it be distributed, that it be articulated. Otherwise it would not become intelligible. I could confine myself to covering it over with vague epithets that would surely not explain clearly what it is. In these conditions, the first term of the alternative tends very much to approximate the second.

We must moreover observe that if my experience succeeds in formulating and consequently communicating itself, it tends by that very fact to change its nature. In fact, I am no longer enclosed by it. I cease to experience the kind of distress which for me is linked to what I cannot account for. In other words it changes its affective coloring. That is not all. If by experience is understood a certain state immediately felt by me, I must unhesitatingly say that *it is not* on experience understood in this restrictive fashion that the certitude I aspire to bears.

Le Peuch, May 1

I do not feel well today. Is that the reason why these latest notes seem to lead nowhere?

However, it is necessary to ask on what the certitude which I am looking for bears. If we wish, it is a matter of finding a meaning in my life. But it will be necessary to add that this meaning cannot satisfy me, that I am unable to recognize it except on condition that this meaning is not exclusively mine. For instance, I could not be satisfied with the certitude which would consist in testifying to the general incoherence and absurdity of the world and of life. However, there is a difficulty here. If I seek the truth and if the last word on reality is precisely not to have any meaning, would I not be bound to be satisfied with this negative assurance? Otherwise, would I not have to admit that what I am seeking is not the truth, but a truth limited to my capacity, a stimulating or consoling truth? Is not this admission my condemnation? That is a difficulty which I must come to close grips with. Must I contest the existence in me of a prejudice, or should I not on the contrary proclaim it?

At any rate, it would be necessary to bring out in the open once and for all the intrinsic absurdity that lies in imagining that any inquiry whatever can lead up to a conclusion on the question of knowing if life has any meaning or not. Moreover, we must affirm in principle that each of us will be able to find as many empirical arguments as he will want in order to convince himself—or to strengthen in himself the conviction—that life has no meaning. But there is some weighing to be done, that is to say, a judgment to be pronounced. For this judgment, something occurs which is out of proportion with a thought that would be satisfied with accumulating charges or grievances. *Acquittal, absolution.* [Jotting from January, 1959: I reproduce these two words without being sure of the precise value I would accord to them and without being certain any longer that they are here in their place.]

Besides, it remains to be asked how this judgment is possible; starting from what type of structure of reality it can be exercised.

We shall also have to ask much more precisely what must be understood by "having a meaning." Briefly, it is a question of making explicit first the exigence which is in us. Can I say for example, as I have done earlier, that this exigence is satisfied when I come face to face with a work in which a life finds at once its expression and its justification? Is there an example or an illustration of a certain universal relation, of an absolute meaning which precisely I am trying to discover? In admitting that the work suffices to confer a meaning on life, it actually seems that this is only the symbolization of something far more essential. But I admit that this is not clear in my mind.

A difficulty which I perceive at this moment is the following: by experience do we understand my experience such as it is given, in an unavoidably imperfect and mutilated fashion, to me who lives it; or else on the contrary do we mean human experience in general? But it seems that from the moment we speak of human experience in general, we cut it off from what makes it experience. It is almost obvious that it can be given only here and now and it manifests a certain characteristic of intransmissibility. Doubtless, there really is an experience (*Erfahrung*) in Kant's sense, which is in process of being constituted and which at bottom tends to be inscribed in an immense catalog that is necessarily

incomplete, like Larousse's monthly. But experience
thus conceived tends not only to exclude all metaphysical significance, but even seems to put the one who is
engrossed in it or devoted in it outside the possibility of
raising the question.

Le Peuch, May 2

After the eclipse of yesterday, I am again seeing more
clearly. I have understood very clearly that it is on the
existential indubitable that everything ought to be centered. I must show that this indubitable can have only
the character of a presence which can be intercepted
(one can also speak of light). I must relate this with
what I wrote the day before yesterday on the presence
to myself. My big mistake has been in not holding on
to the center, just when I had found it, but in continuing haphazard investigations.

I must complete my reflection upon "being in quest
of . . ."

Let us not be beguiled by a grammatical form. We
do not seek something purely and simply; we look for
something *to eat,* or *to use* in a definite manner. To say
that I am in quest of a certitude is not enough. What is
it that I claim to do with this certitude? Perhaps, before
all, to proclaim it. But even this is not enough; for I
have someone in view before whom I will proclaim it.
Would it be myself? Someone for whom it is interesting that this certitude be proclaimed. But interesting in
what way? Is it simply a matter of filling a gap? Surely
not. Will it be necessary to have the notion of power
brought in here? If I have the certitude that such an
event will take place, I can act accordingly. This certitude confers on me a certain power in reference to this
event. I can prepare myself for it, take some precau-

tions, etc. Such a certitude can therefore be possessed
in the sense in which one possesses a means for. . . .
This is also applicable to everything which permits a
determinate category of problems to be resolved. But
here, things are different. A confusion is always possible, however. I am perpetually in danger of losing sight
of this essential difference between a possessed certitude and the existential certitude the character of
which I am trying to define. By essence, the possessed
certitude can be passed on and transmitted. It does not
cling to the one who comes by it. Idea of a certitude by
which one is nourished. Is that only a word? A certitude
which should command a certain interior expansion.
But this is still not clear enough.

Should we not investigate the relation of each of
these types of certitude with the one who formulates
them on the one hand, and with that on which they
bear on the other? Objective certitude tends to depersonalize itself; I am satisfied only on condition that I
am able to say: "It is certain that." It refers to a
structure which I can say is equally that of things or
that of ideas. The case of existential certitude is entirely
different. Here it is not a question of doing away with
the subject but of transforming it. This is still not clear
enough. We would have to make it more concrete, if
necessary by starting from an imperfect illustration: for
example, from the certitude which bears on the love I
feel for another or the other feels for me. Compare to
clouds which prevent me from seeing a certain constellation. But the comparison is misleading, in this sense
that the clouds in question can, by thickening, undoubtedly affect the very *existence* of the constellation.

If I say that the existential certitude bears on the
meaning of life, this will be on condition of taking the
word "meaning" in its non-intellectualistic connota-

tion. I refer to an experience which would be translated fairly precisely by recalling that life dispenses to one sometimes its emptiness, sometimes its fullness.

I am writing this on a Sunday afternoon in a moment of extreme fatigue, of complete aridity, of absolute colorlessness. I am at a dead end.

Le Peuch, May 3

I have the impression that I tend to wander away. Perhaps there is nothing to be retained from the last page. There are, however, some notes of April 30 and May 2 on certitude that I can do something with. The problems stated are essential. What kind of satisfaction do the formulas I am seeking to invent aim at procuring? There is no real difference between my relation to myself which this formulation supposes, and my relation to the other. I try out on myself what is meant for the other, like a doctor who starts out by testing remedies on himself. This comparison is superb. The doctor can experiment on himself only if he has in some degree contracted the illness which he is attempting to cure in others. We must specify clearly what this illness is.

But the doctor can be in a condition which renders this experimentation impossible and sterile. In the same way I can be in a condition which makes it impossible for me to think for the other. I refer especially to a feeling of being inwardly ruffled that I know well. Its effect is to suppress all communion, all intimacy with myself. Yet it is where I am open to myself that it is given to me, not as something additional but by that very fact itself, to be open, to be available to the other. One can detect here the articulation uniting my thoughts on certitude and those on presence.

I must, however, try and bring out better the nature of the certitude thus investigated. I observe that by definition I cannot know exactly what I am looking for. I cannot form an idea of it beforehand; otherwise my search would be without purpose. Some degree of specification is, however, possible. I can proceed by means of an illustration: for example, personal immortality. I try to express for my own benefit, and consequently for the benefit of the other, how it can be conceived. At the basis of this search, is there a simple wish? Undoubtedly, when I wish that such an event take place, I know that my wish does not effect any change in things. Does the same apply here? At first one would be tempted to think so. There is the idea of an objective structure of my being which excludes perhaps the possibility of personal survival: one can compare this with this or that kind of exercise I would like to be able to do, but to which my body is not adapted. On the other hand, must we admit that here [with respect to immortality] the need to affirm *attests* the reality of what is affirmed? Let us say specifically that at the outset I am much less concerned with my own immortality than with that of the beings I love. This connects with what I said about challenge on April 30. "To be in quest of" is to apply oneself to making something take shape that had first been "thrown" or projected. This implies the struggle against an element like water for the one who is working on the construction of a bridge.

Hope, the principle of projection: it must be true that. . . . Anticipation concerning, not the event, but what can be elaborated by an authentic reflection. Anticipation as the transcendent switching of reflection. Being aware at the same time of the forces which anticipation mobilizes against itself: (crystallization in the opposite direction).

Note written on my return from Carennac: *presence is intersubjective.* It cannot but be interpreted as the expression of a will which seeks to reveal itself to me; but this revelation supposes that I do not put an obstacle in its way. In short, the subject is treated, not like an object, but as the magnetic center of presence. At the root of presence there is a being who takes me into consideration, who is regarded by me as taking me into account. Now, by definition, an object does not take me into account; I do not exist for it.

Le Peuch, May 4

Presence as response to the act by which the subject opens himself to receive; in this sense it is the gift of oneself. Presence belongs only to the being who is capable of giving himself.

We probably miss the essential by saying that the [one] subject has to make himself recognized by the [other] subject. Not that this is false, but it is not enough, for what counts here is the initiative which does not emanate from the initial subject. It is at bottom grace or something which is very close to it.

(I should investigate the relation between presence and value. This is far more difficult. I think that there can be an evil presence, and I can welcome this presence into myself like the other.)

It is therefore wholly correct to say with B. that there is no sense in speaking of presence in itself. I must ask myself what an eternal, indefectible presence would be.

But all this ought to be linked with what I wrote on April 30 concerning presence to myself. There is in me something intersubjective, that is to say, some possibilities of intimacy with myself, but also a possible deficiency with regard to this intimacy which can drop almost to zero. I can become wrapped up in myself to the point of no longer communicating with myself at all, much less with others.

Introspection would confuse, or is in danger of confusing, these very sensitive notions. It has nothing to do with the intimacy I am speaking about. To have a penetrating awareness of this or that impulse stemming from my self-esteem for example is not at all to be intimate with myself.

Perhaps it would be fitting to begin with a much more precise examination of the intersubjective in general. For example, I observe one of my household who is busy eating; I am irritated by his slowness or his gluttony: "Will he never have done!" This other is engrossed in his food and pays no attention to me. We are as far apart as we can be. There is no intersubjective bond between us. The other is not present for me: he is simply "this slow poke" or "this glutton." He is not interested in me; it matters very little to him to keep me waiting. What does he care if there is nothing left for me in the dish! A good example of what I yesterday described as the feeling of being ruffled. It is the "where do I figure in this?" that I refer to in my lecture "I and the other."

The possible unity between us is broken both by the fact that the other is too engrossed to take notice of me as well as by the fact that I for my part consider him with irritation and from the outside. The situation is slightly changed if the other perceives that I have long since finished and that I am waiting and if he excuses himself for it. From the moment he takes me into consideration, he ceases to be pure object for myself. Still I must have the impression that he is not merely addressing some words of simple politeness to me.

I copy the postscript of my letter to B.: "I have to

insist on the fact that presence to myself is the necessary condition without which value ceases to be experienced and even recognized. Here I must refer to those states of complete aridity which are entirely compatible with the awareness I feel of being irritated, of being nothing but a wound, a burning wound; one cannot bear the idea of another touching it. This 'Do not touch me' can subsist even when the initial pain has subsided."

A study should be made of the *suspicious consciousness* that would shed light on many contemporary testimonies. The more one is centered on the self—as one is on an ailing organ or an aching tooth—the more is value rejected. At bottom despair is confused with solitude, and there is no value without communion. But these words can be misleading: there is a solitude, that of the great contemplatives, which is a communion; and there are also some pseudo communions which are only alienation. We would need to have in French a scale of words such as exists in English between "solitary," "lonely," "forlorn." The word "isolation" is scarcely of any use, for it implies some degree of nostalgia. Negative solitude, on the contrary, is repulsive: it lies at the basis of refusal.

It is in the light of these remarks that we could take up the question whether truth is subjective. Truth is a value and that is why we can love the truth and suffer or die for it. We should refer to the tragic situations in which we see the truth trampled under foot, for example in the course of a trial or again by charlatans who mutilate their experiences in order to seduce their clientele—and in which we undertake, no matter what the cost, to reinstate to its rights this trampled truth.

It is clear that the truth is not in any way a presence, but also that we can adopt this attitude of the militant witness only on the condition of communicating with ourselves and with an infinity of beings who undoubtedly are symbolized for us by this or that exemplary figure of the master or friend. This is in contrast to the irony of the cynic who witnesses abuses as so many spectacles calculated to reinforce him in his previous nihilism.

The transcendent and unconditional character of value: it is value which determines the conditions.

The property of value is to assume a certain function in relation to life on which it sets its mark. But what exactly do we mean by that? I must not be misled by a metaphor. The notion of consecration intervenes here in two ways: if I consecrate my life to a value, this value in return consecrates it. But this is still very vague.

Let us suppose that I set up as my life's goal the accumulation of riches. I could in principle assume that each one should do the same. Either it is a question of putting at my disposal means as powerful as possible in order to assure me one day of certain pleasures; or else (even if the idea of these pleasures remains in the background) I find my pleasure in this very accumulation: my life finds its meaning in the very act of becoming rich. Shall we say that the act by which an existence so oriented will be judged inferior to a life placed under the aegis of art or science itself has only a wholly subjective bearing? But the question is badly put. One may doubt that it is better to pass one's life smearing paint on canvas than in working to become rich. Despite the intrusion of the word "art," it is not certain that value, in the ultimate meaning of that word, is present in one case rather than in the other. One can also sell a painting like a confectionery without there

being any intrinsic difference between these two trans-
actions.

*Value intervenes only with a certain rigor in the
exigence that one formulates in relation to oneself.* But
this is not yet a solution. Let us take the unsuccessful
artist who has an ideal but does not succeed in realizing
it. It is really only from the ethical point of view that
one would be able to evaluate him. And even then one
can think he has wasted his strength, that he would
have done better to recognize his lack of talent and to
aim less high: by that I mean to renounce art and to
take up an ordinary occupation. It follows from this
that it can be entirely false to attribute to value the
power to justify and ennoble the life of the one who
thinks he is dedicated to it. The example of the unsuccessful artist could not be dwelt upon too deeply. Value
can become the *pretext* from which I set out to try to
justify my existence in my own eyes. The role played by
self-complacency. It is the parody of self-presence. I
note that self-complacency has an affinity with the
feeling of self-pity, about which I have often wondered
without disclosing its nature.

I wonder whether there is not always some pretension in thinking that one is consecrated to value. No
one dares, no one should dare, to say of himself: "I am
at the service of beauty or of truth." This could be said
only by the other and would look terribly like a funeral
oration. The one who is engaged in a certain task,
whatever it be, provided it is an authentic task to which
he devotes himself, will not even have the idea of
defining it in this way, and that, whether he labors in
pain or in joy. Terrible gap between direct testimony
and the philosopher's commentary. The philosopher,
while speaking of the true artist or the true scientist,

ought to refrain from speaking of them as the false artist or the false scientist would speak of himself.

Le Peuch, May 5

Definitely I find the expression "self-presence" is misleading. It is calculated to lead us astray. It would be necessary to find another word but I renounce looking for it for the moment. It would be well to contrast the word "active" with the word "idle": self-complacency is always linked with idleness.

I must reflect on the conditions on which an active consciousness is possible. The image of a tool operating on a certain material in order to shape it up tends to falsify everything. The working consciousness is in no way comparable to a tool, but its action is immanent. I must resume from this point of view the problem of attention. I could take as an example reading, the act which consists in being absorbed in what one reads: there would be a hierarchy to be instituted here. The example of reading is good enough because it lies on the border between the active and the passive. There is a reading which one indulges in only to pass the time: one reads as one would bite one's fingernails. Here there would have to be brought in the notion, so difficult to make clear, of seriousness in contrast to diversion. In one case one devotes oneself completely; in the other one holds oneself back and one diverts a small part of one's strength, that is to say primarily of his attention. It is evident that play for the child is not a pastime. We must ask what exactly is meant by, "having a passion for . . ." or "being captivated by. . . ." One meets perhaps here the single-mindedness of Charles Morgan.

Le Peuch, May 6

I fear that in all this there is some confusion. The notion of seriousness is important; the active consciousness takes seriously what it does, but this is not necessarily to be impassioned.

I do not know if the distinction proposed yesterday can render the services which I expected of it. On the contrary it can be a source of confusion. The contemplative consciousness is surely not a modality of the idle consciousness; but can it be related to the active consciousness? This would oblige us in any case to enlarge the notion and to make it considerably flexible.

I wondered last night if it could not be said that the idea of value has the great inconvenience of transposing to the plane of idle consciousness an implication of the active consciousness, but I do not know if the remark ought to be retained.

The distinction is valuable, at least in as much as it opposes involvement and gratuitousness, but this opposition does not have an absolute character. It contains a whole range, discernible for example in the case of reading, as I have indicated. But in the idea of active consciousness there is something more: there is transformation of a certain content, I would even say that to observe is to work.

Le Peuch, May 7

I have come to a dead end and I am returning to my investigations on fatherhood.

Fatherhood is an essential aspect of the natural order. But nothing is more difficult than to think of the natural order, for generally speaking, it is *by starting from it* that we think. It is taken for granted. We are placed within the necessity of thinking it only from the moment in which this order is put in question. Besides, what engenders the process of reflection is a certain confusion.

What exactly does that mean? I experience confusion when I am suddenly confronted with a situation on which I do not seem to have any hold. Let us add that this situation implies that a certain appeal seems actually to be made to me; but I do not have it in me to respond to it correctly. It is as though I had not been provided with the necessary equipment. In these conditions, I can only indulge in a sort of uncoordinated and ineffective gesticulation which I forthwith renounce because it appears to me vain and ridiculous. I am reduced to hoping that things will work out by themselves, but at the same time the consciousness of the appeal subsists as a discomfort. I cannot come to persuade myself that all this does not concern me. Consequently I am troubled, dissatisfied with myself. It is in vain that I would try to throw the responsibility for this state of things on an external power such as chance, destiny or God.

But in these conditions I would at least be obliged to proceed to a thoughtful scrutiny of the situation and to ascertain whether an appeal has really been made to me, whether I have a responsibility or whether I have been the victim of an error.

Let us apply this to the crisis of paternal authority which is steadily spreading. Its causes are manifold. It undoubtedly corresponds to the development of a sort of anarchic individualism rooted in weakness. But one cannot account for it, I believe, except by starting from a much more central datum which has the character of a loss of consciousness—a consciousness which bears on the specific bond between father and child. Let us observe immediately that the word "bond" here is insufficient and even improper. Actually what is implied here is not a relation. Relation is only an infinitely impoverished and dry logical translation of something which is repugnant to letting itself be conceptualized. It is precisely on the concrete foundations of the relation that the investigation ought to bear; as always in such a case one can proceed only by concentric approaches and often by making an appeal to the negative method which imposes itself especially where we apply ourselves to grasping something transcendent.

It is necessary to refer to concrete situations. The invariance is infinitely more marked in what concerns the relation between mother and child. Here the carnal bond cannot but be deeply felt. What can happen, but in comparatively rare cases, is that the mother experiences toward the child a resentment and so to say a persistent rancor. It is probable that the conditions which tend to prevail in countries partly devitalized contribute to render these anomalies more frequent.

The case of the father is altogether different. His attitude toward the child is actually less directly commanded by the organic realities immediately lived. If we keep to the biological order, in contrast to a definite social order, it is strictly possible for the man to ignore the consequences of the sexual act and to be completely disinterested in them. This remark is important if we want to measure the abyss which separates procreation and paternity. Let us pass on immediately to an extreme case. Let us imagine a man who is put in the presence of an unknown child and through a series of circumstances led to be convinced that this child is his, that is to say that the birth of this child was the result of a short-lived meeting which he scarcely remembers. It could surely happen that, as a result of this discovery, something goes to work in the imagination of this man and also that his affectivity comes into play. But it could also happen that, for hardly honorable motives, he actively sees to it that this activity does not take place within him. Underneath there is the conviction, even though unformulated, that one is a father only if one actually wishes to be and on the other hand that being a father involves responsibilities that it is better not to assume if one is not ready for them.

Here I have envisaged only an extreme case, one that could appear to belong to melodrama rather than to philosophical reflection. Let us now come closer to the data of common experience. Let us take the case of a married couple who have never been eager to have any children and who, perhaps through negligence, have not resorted to any contraceptive measures. A child comes into the world without having been wanted, at least by the father who is worried by the financial burdens which the presence of this undesirable child would impose upon him. On the other hand, because he *does not believe in life*, he is perhaps saddened in a confused sort of way by the coming into the world of this little being who is doubtless bound to have so many disappointments and who will perhaps die in twenty years on some field of battle. Let us endeavor to make the idea that the father has of the bond uniting him with his child emerge in our consciousness. Let us admit that we are dealing with an average person, not one who is inhuman or degenerate. The governing factor is the type of relation existing between the spouses. Doubtless they are united by a solid "egoism of two," the kind which the tandems popular among the working class of 1936 symbolized so well. The child presents itself to the father at first as an intruder; to the mother he will give in proportion as she herself gives, provided she is not degenerate. Of course, if the father is not completely deprived of sensibility, the presence of the child will stir up in him some positive sentiments which will militate against the initial annoyance or exasperation, sentiments tinged with affection, with curiosity, sometimes with pity, sometimes also with pride. But so long as this presence will not have contributed to awaken, in some way retroactively, the wish which normally it should gratify to the full, one can say that the existence of the paternal sentiment will continue to be absent.

While recalling the dreadful hours passed on Meissonnier street during the first months of 1940, I thought of the unfathomable sorrow which is attached to things abandoned by the one who is no longer there, to the remains. Their ontological status would have to be investigated. It is actually as though the abandoned things are in mourning and this sadness is as it were a contagion with which it infects us the survivors.

That there is a sadness in things (let us recall Virgil) it would be wrong to deny. It is commonly admitted that we put it in things, but here my conception of presence as intersubjective shows itself very illuminating. Doubtless this sadness exists for us; one cannot quite say that it comes from us. Our gaiety can suddenly vanish at the sight of a landscape or of a collection of things which gives an impression of desolation. An associationist explanation would be insufficient here.

While meditating on whatever does not cease to weigh me down, I also thought that when we reflect deeply on the conditions of life, they cannot but appear

inacceptable. Life seems to ask us to forget its conditions. It would be necessary to search further in this
direction.

I must call to mind the person who does not leave
any personal belongings behind; a being consumed with
charity; the death of the religious here takes on its full
value and one will understand to what corresponds the
idea of an incorruptible body.

The other day while returning from Sarrazac, A. told
me some interesting things about the image as a simula-
crum. "It is natural," he said, "that one cannot look the
image in the face, place it before oneself as a thing, for
it immediately disappears because it is an artifice permitting consciousness to fool itself. "Now, one cannot
be at the same time the one who is fooled and the one
who fools." There is some truth in that, but it still has
not been made fully clear.

I am not sure that the image is an artifice. Note that
it is in itself incommunicable, it must become a thing
in order to be transmitted to the other. It is therefore
linked to solitude; it is the fruit of a solitary consciousness. This is only the beginning.

There is however a meaning, or what I have said is
false. The image is a way of remaining occupied by
what is no longer there. Perhaps we should start with
the haunted house in order to understand. I mean that
perhaps there is no essential difference between the
haunted place and the man obsessed by an image. In
the two instances one is in the presence of a connivance
which is at bottom unintelligible. But this is still not
sufficiently relevant.

Note of last May 3 clarified by that of June 1, 1942.
Why does it seem to us at first absurd to think that our
inner attitude in relation to a missing person can exert
an influence upon him? But the word *influence* is bad. I

must find another one for it. The reason is that one remains hypnotized by the idea that the other is essentially a thing outside of our reach and which depends only on techniques that are applicable to the world of things (exhumations, analyses, etc.). As for the living, thinking being, he no longer exists at all: I keep a selection of mental photographs of him and that is all. I am privileged to look at them and while doing so to feel such and such a sentiment of regret, tenderness, etc. But in the light of presence, everything is transformed. The presence of a missing person was not a presence in the instant; it was not that of a spectacle but that of a being, that is to say, that it implied on my part an engagement. This engagement was, moreover, linked to the fact that I opened myself to this being in order to welcome him. Here, however, at this moment, the thread is broken. We must see later if I succeed in taking it up again.

Perhaps it is more instructive to ask on what condition it would be conceivable that this action on the missing person could be exercised. We would have to admit not only or even essentially that he is still there—for it is not really clear what that means—but that we remain united beyond what it is given to my consciousness to grasp. We should try and understand of what kind such a unity could be and at the same time why it is not immediately apprehended.

We must consider fatherhood in terms of self-love. There is a good and a bad love of self. The latter tends to prevail. Self-love is not necessarily egoism. There is even an egoism which is a disgust for self.

The love of self can be the love of a family line of which one recognizes oneself to be the transitory and imperfect representative. From this point of view, it is not a question of reproducing oneself but of continuing a momentum. Egoism, on the contrary, is absolutely limited: one is no more than an atom which seeks the maximum possible enjoyment and the least possible suffering. From this point of view what does fatherhood become? But it is not necessary to dwell too long at the aristocratic idea of the family line. Each of us, however modest be our origins, can have the awareness of an infinite delegation of which he is the object. The individual atom ignores them and does not know itself as wanted.

Le Peuch, May 9

Start from the fact that, from the organo-psychic point of view, fatherhood has none but weak foundations. It is from the sociological point of view that it can be solidly established. It must also be added that here the sociological awareness is inseparable from a certain metaphysical awareness. If the latter weakens, then automatically the experience of fatherhood tends to become problematic.

Le Peuch, May 10

I would like to put in order the notes taken during these last weeks in order to prepare the kind of profession of faith which Jean Grenier requested from me for the collective work on existence to be published by Gallimard.[1]

I am not merely in search of a certitude *here and now* at this precise moment at which I write. This has always been true ever since I came to a certain level of awareness. Besides, it is difficult for me to say exactly

---

[1] This collective work has appeared, but I decided not to contribute my text. It has remained unpublished until this day.

how this coming to this level of awareness has taken
place. I recall however in the most precise way the role
played in this awakening, not by the idea of my death,
but by the fact of the death of a being infinitely close;
for in a certain sense, this fact governed my life to its
very depths.

The myth of Orpheus and Eurydice is in this sense at
the very heart of my existence. The essential problem
has always been, and still is for me to know how we can
meet again—if only in hope. What then is this hope?
How does it not only take shape, but justify itself, give
an account of itself?

I must reflect, however, on what is this indefatigable
search to which I have been devoted myself for a third
of a century. Can I in all conscience say that I know
what I am looking for? If I do, it seems that I am no
longer seeking. If not, how can I seek? There is an
antinomy there which arises only for a certain type of
search. If I am looking for a lost object it is evident that
the question does not arise. I know the thing I am
looking for. I can give a description of it and I would be
able to recognize it. The antinomy does not exist where
the research bears on a thing, or on a being comparable
to a thing, which it is a question of recovering. I am
justified in positing in principle that this being or this
thing is somewhere; it is a question of finding out
where. However, a distinction needs to be made. Is it
not possible that there exists a thing so exactly like that
one I am looking for that it is indistinguishable from it?
In these conditions it can happen that I am mistaken
and that in believing I had found the lost thing I put
my hand on that which does not let itself be distinguished from it. Common sense will remark that this
amounts to the same and that this other thing will as
well answer the purpose. It is not certain that I will be

so accommodating. If a certain irreducible value is for me attached to the individual existence of what I am looking for, I would resist with scorn the idea of a possible equivalence. The idea of this confusion is intolerable to me; I see in it as it were a betrayal or a sacrilege with respect to what is actually in question, that is to say the ipseity. (This will become clear if we take as an example an object which has been given to me by a dear friend.)

However this remark, important though it be, does not directly throw light on the search to which I proceed as a metaphysician. The latter surely does not bear on a thing nor on anything whatever which can be treated as a thing.

But one may ask: does this research not belong to the order of invention? The notion of invention, however, is equivocal. It is relatively clear only where it is a question of imagining a procedure for obtaining a result that is precise and objectively determinable. The artist is not an inventor. Here I call to mind the art with which I am familiar, the dramatic art. Invention intervenes only secondarily where it is a matter of finding a means for realizing a certain end, for example in order that two characters meet, or in order that one of them may learn, or, on the contrary, remain ignorant of this or that fact, etc. Invention belongs to the category of what in itself is not invention but creation. But we may wonder whether this pure creation is not of the same order as the inquiry that I am here striving to think about. When I create, I can say neither that I *know* nor that I am purely and simply ignorant of where I am going. My creation cannot be effected on the basis of a pure and simple desire to create. The desire is in itself sterile; it is only an *I would like*. But it is necessary that something be *present* to me: a character, a situation, a relation, but nothing that can be reduced to an abstract idea. However ingenious it be, the abstract idea is sterile. Creation is essentially a germination, and it is very difficult not only to know to what extent I can contribute to the development of the initial germ, but also what this question precisely means. It does not seem indeed that I am able to make precise the relation that links the "I" to this germ which is present to me. This whole process organizes itself in relation to a work which will have to possess a certain form. What counts is to produce this work which will have to exist by itself and impose itself not only on me but on others.

Does the same thing apply here? Let us not lose sight of the fact that for me it is a question of arriving at a certitude. Undoubtedly this latter will have to take shape in writing and be able to be communicated. But what is important is this certitude itself. It is here the point of arrival, whereas for the dramatist it is a departure (I must be sure of my character, of his relationships, etc.); as such, this certitude is already distinct from what I have called the germ.

But in the present case that of philosophic inquiry, what is meant by certitude? It even seems necessary to distinguish between *the* certitude and *a* certitude as between *the* truth and *a* truth. In the present case, it is *the* certitude with which we are concerned. How can I go about looking for it?

Let us first ask ourselves what it is to seek for a particular certitude. It is to put in operation certain proven methods in order to reach an optimum point from where I shall see what is actually concealed from me. Let us not, however, be deceived by the word "to see" or rather let us not take it in its literal meaning. The fact remains that when I have reached this point, what I am looking for will have *to appear to me*. Such an inquiry entails an aspect of invention. I will almost certainly have to devise methods which permit me to arrive at this optimum position, or again to construct the observatory in which I intend to place myself. It is of the essence of *a* certitude that it should bear on a "problematizable" content, that is to say giving rise to questions which would occur for anyone who finds himself in a given situation. For example, an astronomical certitude will refer to a certain constellation contemplated by an inhabitant of earth who is led to wonder at what distance this constellation is situated from him.

Does *the* certitude to which I aspire display this characteristic? It appears to be global; but what do we mean by that? Do we mean that the particular certitudes are to *the* certitude what coins would be in relation to the ingot from which they are derived? Far from it, for on reflection there appears to be no homogeneity between *the* certitude and particular certitudes. When I ask *to what* does the certitude refer I certainly cannot answer. If, for instance, I say that it refers to being, this reply awakens doubts in me. Nay more, I am not even sure that it is legitimate to ask the question. For it seems that ultimately certitude is indistinguishable from its object.

Here, however, the initial antinomy reappears. How can I reach this certitude? A deeper reflection will have to be made.

Is not this certitude which I am looking for only the means of expressing, that is of rendering communicable to myself and the other, a certain assurance which lies deep within me? Or is it this assurance itself that I am seeking to obtain? In this second case it is for me first a matter of realizing a change in my way of situating myself with respect to, let us say, the reality itself. In the first case, however, this change will be neither necessary nor perhaps possible.

The examination of this alternative compels us to investigate the nature of this eventual distinction which we will have to make subsequently between a fundamental assurance and the act by which it would be made known and justified.

First another possibility must be taken note of. Can it not be said, with the adversaries of every *consoling* metaphysics, that I intend to prove to myself what I wish for? Here we would have to investigate the nature and the conditions of the possibility of this fundamental *wish*. In what case is it certainly illegitimate to mistake one's desires for realities and especially to treat them as such?

Desire refers to something external to myself which I would like to possess. It can be applied to all the modalities of having. I must avoid being taken in and to add up what I have and what I do not have. It remains to be seen if the aspiration within me which aims at certitude can be compared to a desire. It seems that it may belong rather to the order of hope.

Le Peuch, May 12

When we censure thought for prejudging the result of an inquiry, we postulate that it should observe in reference to being and non-being a neutrality comparable to that of the scientist. When the scientist proceeds to an experiment he is forbidden to speculate in advance on what it will yield.

But there is every reason to believe that this comparison is illegitimate and that the neutrality in reference to being and non-being is precisely impossible. Does this simply mean that a choice is imposed, that it is

necessary to prefer the one or the other? That means
that it is necessary always to be involved and to make a
decision. I do not have any reason to deny that at the
basis of my inquiry there has always been an option for
being. Moreover, it might be advisable to make concrete and to define what I have rejected. But at the
same time it would be necessary to make a frontal
attack on the idea that what I have rejected is perhaps
the truth. Let us observe that in this case what permits
the evaluation is the fact that each one has known
moments in which he has been tempted to affirm *universal meaninglessness*.

Consequently, what reply must we give to the initial
question as to what we must understand by being certain? It seems *equally false* to say that it is merely to
express what one has always known, and that it is to
arrive at an entirely new way of being. Better to say
that the inquiry here supposes an involvement starting
from a forefeeling. It is also very doubtful that this
forefeeling can be regarded as a modality of knowledge.

On the other hand, one cannot abstract from the
question of knowing what we intend to do with this
certitude. It is not enough to say that we propose
essentially to proclaim it; for, if we do proclaim it, it is
for others that it must be presumed to have interest,
and it is the nature of this interest that we must seek to
elucidate. Does it suffice to say that it will dispel
doubts, anguishes? But this interpretation is wholly
negative. One can consider doubt (or anguish) to be a
negation; or, more precisely, that it comes to interpose
itself between us and a positive good to which we
aspire, a good whose nature we do not define in conceiving it as pure repose. Note that the notion of repose
is one of the most equivocal ones. In certain cases
repose is conceived as pure cessation of fatigue and of

pain; in others, and in a more profound way, one finds in it the presentiment of a recuperation, thanks to which we recover our integrity. Unquestionably one would prefer to speak here of beatitude.

Le Peuch, May 13

Is there not a danger here of causing a serious confusion between metaphysics and religion? We seem to be in presence of a dilemma. Either certitude is confused with salvation in the religious sense of this word, in that case metaphysics loses all autonomy and in the end all reality; or else salvation is on the contrary reduced to certitude, and one falls a prey to an intellectualism of which the doctrine of Spinoza or that of Hegel are the most accomplished expression. But does not Spinoza, like Hegel, make short shrift of the human condition in its specific character?

Le Peuch, May 14

I am not sure whether I will not have to omit this kind of digression. We must resume the relation between myself and certitude, or perhaps more precisely between existing and being certain. Undoubtedly we must here oppose certitude to conviction. Properly speaking, I am not attempting here to form a conviction. Let us note that conviction always comes at the end of an inquiry; there is no conviction where no inquiry is conceivable. Revelation is the opposite of inquiry, and I am not taking this word in its specifically religious sense.

Nevertheless, if I have not tried to form a conviction must we not say simply as we did earlier that I have limited myself to formulating a connected group of prejudices? Here again it seems that there is a dilemma. We could get out of it only on condition of proceeding to a critique of the idea of prejudice, and particularly of making clear the difference between prejudice and hypothesis. Suppose I nurture a prejudice concerning a person whose acquaintance I am about to make. This prejudice is a preconceived idea which I have perhaps formed through the spirit of contradiction for the sake of going against the opinion which I have heard expressed about this person. This prejudice will reveal itself as such by the fact that it will not submit itself to the critique of experience. In some way experience will have to accommodate itself to the prejudice, allowing itself to be trimmed and cut arbitrarily. In short, the prejudice is by its essence tyrannical, which the hypothesis in principle is not.

But is this not precisely the way in which I have behaved with respect to reality as a whole, or to the world? Could I not be reproached for having systematically dismissed everything that was capable of militating against an idea of a totality? Prejudice is tyrannically exercised within a sphere in which there should be room only for hypotheses and in which it pertains to experience to decide. But from the moment in which we are in the presence of transcendence, in whatever way the latter may appear to us, this ceases to be the case. On the other hand, does there not exist between presence and transcendence an intimate correlation? Can we not say that there is no presence (or that it does not manifest itself) except in absence or through absence and that it is precisely in this that transcendence consists in?

We would therefore have to say that presence is not immediate. But immediately we would have to add that if we call it mediate we risk thinking it to be *inferred.* That would amount to saying that it does not reveal itself and that it is therefore not presence.

Basically it is on the *"revealing itself to"* that reflection ought to bear. One might say that this revelation can be accomplished only if I *am emptied of myself.* This is not necessary for the child, who seems here to be the beneficiary of a grace.

In this perspective one will be tempted to say that existence is perhaps an obstacle to revelation (I am tempted to say that the latter is brought about by means of the "air holes" of existence. But is this true?) For existence is above all opacity. I would say that to exist is to seal off. Note, moreover, that opacity does not disappear in becoming conscious of itself. On the contrary the consciousness which is centered on itself is opacity in the highest degree. Opacity to what if not to presence.

But this still does not satisfy me. I must go into this much more closely.

Le Peuch, May 15

What I wrote yesterday needs to be qualified. Is it legitimate to say that to exist is to seal off? To seal off what and for whom?

Le Peuch, May 17

It seems that what is sealed off is a power of making everything fluid, a power of universal transmutation. For whom does this obturation occur?

But I really feel that the question is badly put and that we are caught in the worst confusion.

To apprehend myself as existing is in some way to apprehend myself as captive. My existence is in this respect the sum total of my constraints. True, I am forced to acknowledge that in a certain sense, without these constraints I would be nothing; I would lose my identity. But in another sense, this identity exasperates me and I have a disgust for it. Hence there is a contradiction which I do not completely eliminate when I remember that it is still the basis of this identity that I repudiate. This merely accentuates a twisting around of myself which is an essential aspect of my condition.

All this scarcely satisfies me. But there is something to be retained from the notes of May 14, something which I would like to bring into focus. What is revealed to me in some way *passes right through* everything from which I shall be obliged to separate and free myself in order to attain it. I become immediate for the other who in these conditions ceases to be pure other: the opposition between the self and the other is transcended or reduced. It is in the light of these remarks that one would have to understand what I said about presence within absence. For a better grasp, it would be necessary to refer to the common experience of blindness through familiarity. I cease to see those with whom I live in as much as this life in common consists in a routine of actions and reactions due to living together. In this respect, my near and dear ones are not present to me. Here I refer to certain expressions of Daniel in *The Heart of Others* when he says to Rose that she is not someone else. In order that I see the other it will be necessary that something puts him at a distance from me: the moral phenomenon of farsightedness. Concerning the role which death can play in this context, by removing the other, it separates him from me; it puts him at a distance where I can finally see him, where he can reveal himself to me. But the difficulty for us is that what is present is what acts. But here, does not death make an image of the other for me, an image which doubtless I can contemplate, but which if it is no more than an image can no longer do anything for me? We thus fall back into the difficulties examined some weeks ago.

We must certainly beware of the ambiguity that is attached to the idea of action. To be sure there is a kind of action which is possible only where there is contact, that is to say at the level where we do not see one another. One can say in principle that it is not on this plane that the other, when he is distanced from me, is capable of acting on me or in me. But it would be a begging of the question to say that there is no action except at the level of contact. Instead must we not rather think that in revealing himself to me the other somehow draws me to himself; and that, on condition that I consent to it, he lifts me out of this world where I tended to be only a thing among other things? It is difficult to see how, if the other were reduced to his image, he could accomplish this uplifting or this conversion of myself. When I say: this is only an image, I judge in the name of the affirmation by which I decree that things alone are real in as much as they exist: we behave like things, my friends and I, in so far as we simply adjust ourselves to one another or mutually seek to exploit one another for our personal gain.

Does all this shed light on my obscure formula: to exist is to seal up? In a confused sort of way seems to me that we would also have to speak of the bi-polarity of existence. I must connect what I have just remarked concerning existence as a thing and what I said previously about the degraded everyday life. The connection appears to be as clear as it can be.

I seem to have made progress on the 14th and today.

I have made a kind of discovery in understanding that there can be no revelation so long as we live in a world in which there is friction which we escape only through automatization. Now, it is scarcely an exaggeration to say that such is the character of the world of everyday life. At any rate everyday existence tends almost inevitably to constitute around itself a similar world in contrast to a "paradise": what is intercepted in existence at this level is the light in which paradise is steeped.

Could we not say that this very power of revelation intervenes when I am called upon to see myself and consequently to transcend myself, to reject myself as I am, or again to recognize as an obstacle what seemed to be the very element that I did not cease to inhale?

Le Peuch, May 19

I must take up again the idea according to which a prior obligation of neutrality would exist for a thought which confronts the real. For it is by reason of this obligation that I can be accused of cheating.

Here the comparison with what I said concerning the desire implied in fatherhood is instructive. To behave as father is passionately to side for life; it is not to hold back and expect that experience will teach us whether the new being is viable or not. Besides, it depends on us to a degree that we are unable to appreciate exactly that this being may be in reality viable. Someone will say that here the matter is different because it is a question for thought to recognize what are the characteristics that belong to reality. Thereby one sets up a duality between the thought which recognizes and the reality which is to be recognized. Reflection must inquire in what zone and on what condition this duality can be really maintained. A typical case is that of the scientist who conducts an experiment, who for example puts two things together in order to see what result will follow.

One can also think about the prejudicial neutrality, about the basic impartiality which is maintained by the one who wants to form an opinion of someone by studying his conduct. But it is really necessary to see that it is not in the course of this investigation that he will discover or invent the values according to which he will judge this conduct; these values can only be presupposed.

Or else we can imagine the opposite case, that in which, while having an absolute and prior trust in someone, I would form a system of values based on his conduct, affirming beforehand that what he does is good. But what it is essential to see is that these two possibilities are not only distinct but incompatible. From that we should draw the conclusion that it is absurd to claim to reconcile a metaphysical with a moral agnosticism. I would like to try and express this more clearly. Let us admit that by putting myself in presence of the universe, or rather, absurd though it seem, by attempting to make it appear before me, I am in some way investigating its case. In other words, I am attempting to pass judgment upon it, to discern whether it is the good or the bad that is preponderant in it. I can proceed to this investigation only on condition that I judge myself to be in possession of the categories in reference to which I claim to measure the universe. This is as true in Schopenhauer as in Leibniz. If on the other hand I abandon myself to the universe (or to the supreme principle which is incarnate in it) within a movement of trusting adoration, I shall count on it for directing my judgment. But if I claim to

question all the values and *at the same time* the very
reality of the universe—reality here being confused
with intelligibility in the full sense—in short, if while
proclaiming my own weakness I declare in the same
breath that the world is perhaps absurd, I take my
stand on this side of every judgment and every possible
thought and there is no conjuring trick which permits
me to get out of this desperate situation. Even that is
saying too little. For the property of any situation consists in being able to be exposed or defined. This is
what my situation, it seems, cannot be; for all
the landmarks are lacking. There is no point of reference.

Le Peuch, May 20

In short, I can condemn myself in the name of the
world or I can at most condemn the world in the name
of what I demand, that is of myself. But to pronounce
these two condemnations at the same time is no longer
to think anything at all. More precisely, I appear to
myself as incarnating certain values or at least as har-
boring certain demands. I can recognize that what I
call the world seems incapable of satisfying these demands for justice or even for truth. From this point of
view I condemn the world, but I cannot at the same
time declare these exigencies as void of meaning. The
two condemnations would annul each other.

I am not sure that all this gets us very far. It would
be better to try and define what is the attitude that is
opposed to what I have called the prejudicial neutrality
of thought.

Le Peuch, May 21

I have the impression of roaming across some brush-wood, around an evidence which it would be necessary to reach directly: blinded evidence like a fountain covered with dead leaves.

Le Peuch, May 22

Going back to prejudicial neutrality, I would like to point out that it is conceivable only in a situation which excludes involvement. I do not think that this neutrality is conceivable or rather justifiable in marriage for example, in which each of the partners has to feel in some way responsible for the other, and not only for the happiness of the other. Now, the bond that unites us to the world in which we have to live is in some sense nuptial.

Le Peuch, May 23

Referring to that concluding part of the notes of May 10, I shall say that this search almost inevitably tends to be degraded and translated instead into the language of covetousness and possession. The reference to the transcendent has precisely for its essential function to rectify this deformed image. This is very important.

In reading over my notes of these last weeks, I again recognized distinctly that the question of presence to the self or of intimacy with the self is a key question. It cannot be admitted that it is impossible to arrive at clarity in this question. But I am convinced that I have still not succeeded in stating it in adequate terms.

It is really necessary to begin again with the idea

which I expressed before, according to which I make myself a shadow for myself; therein lies my opacity.

Paris, May 31

Following the conversation which I had yesterday in Fontenay with Jean Grenier, I continue my notes on the metaphysical import of experience. Note that it can be only appreciated but not evaluated. (It has that in common with the esthetic quality; yet it is necessary to add that the latter is attached to a thing on which it sets a price, at least in principle, on a certain market. Nothing of the kind here.)

To what extent can that metaphysical import be appreciated by the one who himself lives his experience? It can be done only with very great difficulty, for the act by which the experience tends to appreciate itself is in danger of reducing it to zero according as this act tends to turn this experience into a pretentious claim; here any such claim is vain and is condemned as soon as it is formulated.

A life inhabited by hope. But can hope too degrade itself (I shall have my *place*—a place which will not be mediocre)?

A life which opens on heaven: but precisely the life of the pretentious bigot does not open on heaven. The latter is confused with the "county theatre" where everybody fights to get a front seat. (It is not for us to say up to what point the door is open since we are ourselves of the earth.)

Prisoners of the "everyday": but we are that only if we are not conscious of being so, if we are comfortably installed in it. It must be added that what is opposed to this installation is not in any way the escape from the everyday life or even the irritation against it; but it is the aptitude for going through it with the eyes fixed elsewhere. But what is this elsewhere? What is heaven? A ritualization of the everyday life is possible, but the latter can itself be degraded when it is not ordained to the transcendent. This reference is in no way comparable to a subjective disposition which would be only a coloring substance. Wherever the subjective disposition exists it is interpreted as the sign of a soul inhabited by hope.

There are ties which are no burden, but which leave intact a certain liberty of life. Close link with availability. The unavailable person is chiefly the one who does not have the time, who is too *busy*. . . .

I hope for you. It is not enough to say that you remain present to me. I do not separate you from myself, and what is not for you cannot be for me either. *Agapē* lies at the root of hope.

Perhaps it is more false to consider heaven as a state than to look upon it as a place. Perhaps too this opposition is fictitious.

Paris, June 1

To understand what the burden of existence is—how the latter is separated from life and tends to be opposed to it. The idea of a defensive armor which is built around some pleasures to which one clings (for nothing in the world would I miss my Tuesday game of bridge, or my weekly session chamber music, etc. . . . Pile-work on top of nothingness).

I must reflect on what the lives which lack these pilings are.

Coagulation which is the sign or the mark of a loss of

sensitivity. This loss of sensitivity corresponds to a general devaluation of life. That is how life degenerates into existence.

Perhaps we can start from that in order to understand what value is. The kind of existence I have just envisioned tends to be constituted on this side of all authentic value in so far as value is linked to creativity.

Compare value to breath or to light: contrast with the stagnant and the pale.

Loss of sensitivity is explained by growing inaptitude for admiration. I must show how admiration deteriorates in a world given over to the domination of technology. Nature compared to a tamed beast. Whatever is good happens in spite of it and in a sense against it. It is a matter of wresting from life the means for making it liveable. One no longer thinks of attributing to it anything that resembles a benevolent complicity.

In addition to what I have said about coagulation, I must indicate the role of covetousness. People live on credit and as it were in the conditional, *while waiting*. At the very most one hopes to get one's chance.

Notes of January 17, 1959

In reading over these notes of Spring, 1943, and those of the following summer, I could not fail to be struck by the contrast of perspectives! In all that precedes, the emphasis is placed primarily on the sealing-up quality of existence, the latter being considered in its opaqueness. On the other hand in the Journals which are going to follow the attention is centered more on what precedes this opaqueness, what by contrast is a bursting forth, or in other words, an exclamation. From this point of view it is interesting to note the difference in resonance between existential and existent. The existent, as the very sound of the word indicates, is the subdued; it is already almost the mortified. By contrast, the clear sound of existential corresponds to the moment of discovery; one could almost say to the moment in which existence is attained or apprehended as *thou*.

This remark, which I think is extremely important, ought to permit us to understand how the reflections which are going to follow are really complementary to the preceding ones.

Le Peuch, August 2, 1943

The existent presents itself to me as something that withstands destruction for a time. Consequently, the existent is what is *still* existing but will one day exist *no more*. This is particularly clear with respect to human artifacts. The house in which L. was born still exists or exists no more. Moreover, the destruction is in some degree presented as immanent in the existent. What exists is imperceptibly destroyed under our eyes.

Here the existent is treated as an object. It can be characterized, but this characterization is relative to the existence and does not define it, existence presenting itself as a sort of test undergone or lived (idea of a resistance offered to this destruction from within). This test is conceived as the extrapolation of an interior struggle going on in the very heart of the agent which is incarnate in the existent thing (as though this struggle was going on, but in a quiet and subdued manner, within the thing itself). Of course, this or that natural reality (a mountain, a rock, etc.) could easily be compared to a human artifact.

From this point of view existence cannot in any way be detemporalized. To exist is to go through a desperate struggle within time. On the other hand what becomes here of the traditional opposition between essence and existence? The struggle has for its stake the maintenance or the disappearance of a certain form. When the form is no longer in any way discernible, the thing no more exists. In other words, the connection between the name and what it claims to designate is no longer guaranteed; the designation survives the designated thing. (But this is only the existence seen and appreciated from the outside; cf. notes of August 14, 1943.)

One will be tempted to say that the more complex an existent is, the more vulnerable it is and the more it lays itself open to destruction; the more elementary it is the less destructible it is: it *already* is what the destruction could make of it. It excludes destruction as a possibility. But such an existent is as though it did not exist. It is characterized by nothing: but to exist is to be characterized; it is to make an appeal to the act of discrimination.

I must inquire what the foundation for this complexity is in the agent himself, and subsequently, whether this agent can be said to exist without a serious ambiguity: problem of the existence of the other and of myself.

But, independently of the difference in complexity, are we not justified in bringing in a difference which has to do with what could be called the degree of belonging to the world? Moreover, it is possible in the last analysis that these two distinctions approximately coincide. Let us say that a being endowed with intelligence and heart presents a great many points that insert him into the world. His belonging to the world is infinitely richer than that of the being devoid of intelligence and completely lacking in sensibility. What is the relation between existence and belonging to the world?

Perhaps it would be fitting to ask ourselves first in what sense it is legitimate to say that determinations like *still* or *no longer* truly affect existence or the existent. When I say: such a picture no longer exists, I mean that it no longer forms part of the actually given world. Consequently I must renounce the hope of seeing it, and I must no longer expect to see it included in an exhibition of the works of its author. If some photographs or copies of it exist, one can, through the one or the other, still "form the idea" of it, even though the thing itself no longer exists. Or if there are still some people who saw it before it was destroyed, one can still form a vague idea of it through their description. Shall we say that in these conditions it still exists, although to a lesser degree? I do not think so. It no longer exists (this would indicate the solidarity between existence and ipseity), it has existed, it has belonged to this world but no longer is a part of it. Can we say that it still leads a posthumous, starry existence in the memory of those who have seen it and who remember it? Here the central difficulties appear. What is this "it"? Must we admit that this "it" is the essence of the picture, that this essence has first existed, but that while no longer existing, it survives in some way in the memory of these art lovers? The process of destruction could have been exercised only on the existent, not on the essence itself.

But is there not a secondary process of destruction which attacks the brain cells of these art lovers who themselves before long will no more exist (just like the photographs or copies, too, are bound to disappear in the long run)?

But one can wonder if all that is not artifical, if one is not arbitrarily given the idea of an essence which would have preceded its own incarnation and which somehow would be able to outlive it by a rather precarious survival. Now everything leads us to think that the painting comes into existence only in its being materialized. Only in a roughly approximate way can we claim that it pre-existed itself. Likewise the image that the one who contemplated it before keeps of it is neither the painting nor the essence of the painting; it is only a sort of imperfect way to refer to it.

Le Peuch, August 3, 1943

Here it seems to me that we should distinguish between the case of beings and that of things. Let us take up that of beings [persons] first.

Even if the being whose disappearance I mourn in a sense no longer exists, he still exists for me—must I say: *by the fact that he has existed?* It can no longer happen that he does not exist. We therefore have a vexing contradiction, the terms of which we must explore. He no longer exists; he is no longer of this world; he no longer has a share in it. One will no longer have to consult him (but although this is true of the [impersonal] "one," it is perhaps not true of *me*: there is possibility of a personal appeal, of an entreaty). "One" will no longer therefore take him into consideration. He is excluded from the universal reckoning. (However, this is not even legally true, to the extent that his will is taken into consideration; but the latter belongs to the still existing, if it is recorded in writing.)

If it is permissible to speak of promotion within existence—we must ask ourselves what that means exactly—it all goes to show that this promotion can be accomplished only by means of a *conspiracy*. Nothing therefore can be further from the truth than to imagine a sort of transposition of the essence into existence which would automatically take place through the pure and simple efficacy of powers immanent in the essence. An analogous inquiry will have to be made as to whether another form of conspiracy is not required for keeping in existence the person whom we believe at first withdrawn from the world or from existence (contradiction pointed out further back). This original conspiracy is organized around a being of whom one still does not know anything, of whom there is still nothing to know, but who concentrates on himself the loving solicitude of those who hope in him. The essence of this being consists in the prophetic hope which he awakens.

Can it be conceived that this being who has been all future will one day be only all past? What would this imply metaphysically? That would amount to affirming for me or for us the metaphenomenal character of this existence which according to us subsists, even though existence pure and simple has ceased. "According to us," I say, for the property of this existence is not to be manifest; it is a secret and we are loath to surrender this secret to a stranger; in other words, to profane it. Perhaps we who are the holders of this secret will explain our experience fairly precisely if we say that we keep watch while someone is sleeping. This amounts to saying that we hope that this person will wake up. To keep watch while someone is sleeping is in some way to see to it that sleep is not troubled or interrupted by intruders. But in this case from what intrusion do we have to protect those whom we love? This intrusion can be none other than infidelity in all its aspects, of which forgetting or negligence or even indiscretion is the most common. I do not think I have written anything which more directly explains a most intimate and constant experience. But this is still only a beginning.

It is necessary to note that a divergence of interpretation can occur between us, the holders of the secret, when one of us sees only infidelity in a memory, whereas the other has the intimate conviction that what is betrayed is the reality itself, the existent. How can this divergence of interpretation occur and what is its scope?

If that is possible it is because we are no longer in *the domain of existence as such,* in which an inquiry that permits verification is always possible at least in principle. To resume and extend the metaphor mentioned above, everything happens as if this sleep was contemplated through a transparent partition. We are not in a condition to assure ourselves if this sleeper still breathes. He has been removed from our grasp. We are no longer in any way permitted to indulge in any kind of detective manipulation of him that would provide the means for us to make a statement about his real state. More precisely, this manipulation can no longer be exercised except on a likeness in process of disappearing (exhumation of a body). Moreover, this image is imposed upon us and it is only on condition of triumphing over the obsession which emanates from it that we can keep our secret and respect the vow which is inseparable from it.

But the one who is content with respecting a memory yields in the last analysis to the power of intimidation which emanates from the likeness. This is because he ends by considering the latter as the reality, of which the only thing left for us to do is to preserve in ourselves a copy that fades day by day—as one dusts a photograph above the fireplace. However, this is only the rather deceptive representation which one makes to oneself of what is essentially an act of worship. One experiences the need for accomplishing and renewing this act; but at the same time, one feels one is unable to conceive it. In the last analysis, nothing can be explained here from the point of view of the image alone. Even if it is the image, material or immaterial, that I take care of or hold on to, it is only *out of love for the being himself*. This amounts to saying that *the latter is not treated as an image*. Otherwise we shall be driven to absurdity. Our fidelity can be based only on a sustained adherence or application to an existence which cannot in any way be relegated to a world of images. All that one can say is that an image, however rudimentary it be, is necessary for me in order that I can become aware of this adherence or this application. It is the modality according to which this adherence or application takes on a significance for me. Let us say provisionally that the memory shows details in images; it is retailed under the form of images without being itself an image.

It does not seem that this last point can be seriously contested. However, it contains an ambiguity. Should not this existence to which I continue to adhere be affirmed as a simple *past* existence (a continuing existence of what no longer exists)? But this formula is ambiguous. It seems that we may have to distinguish very strictly here:

1. the persistence of the past as past, as recalled;

2. an indefectible principle by attachment to which we entertain these memories.

There is everything to lose in imagining that this indefectible principle is itself image or memory; it is a sustained presence. The being I love continues to be there. He is there even as I am and by the same right. I am only by reason of the connection maintained with him, and if this link were broken, I would no longer be.

But the strange, infinitely paradoxical thing is that this indefectible principle may be covered over and stifled by these memories and that the latter in being substituted for it become idols.

From this point of view there would be no sense in claiming that the indefectible principle belongs to the past; such belongingness would ruin this indefectibility. A conditional indefectibility, some will say; not so, but given (ascertainable) only for the one who, I shall not say has rendered himself worthy of it, but demands it in the utmost depth of himself.

The indefectible is what cannot be wanting where a radical fidelity is maintained. This amounts to saying that it is *a response*. But at the same time this response cannot be automatic without the fidelity being altered and even destroyed in its principle. This is the same as saying that the faithful soul must have the experience of the "night" and even that it must recognize the temptation of letting itself be blinded interiorly by this night which it is obliged to go through. This experience is linked to the everday life as such, to the "day after day." The indefectible is therefore not at all the permanence of an essence, or at least it is not according to the mode of such a permanence that it can be granted to us; for whatever the essence it is infallibly disclosed to a thought which progresses according to a certain objectively formulable law. Here there is no such thing; there can be nothing of the kind when it is a being-to-being relationship that is in question. For that very reason there cannot be a technique of love or of charity. From the side of the subject, however, where any technique is inconceivable, there is room for all kinds of gaps, for all kind of false moves, for every kind of abuse and forgery.

It is through these innumberable errors and vicissitudes that it is given to us to see the *intermittent fires of the indefectible* shine. I do not conceal the fact that there is apparently something contradictory in joining intermittence to indefectibility. But it is precisely this paradoxical union that we should be able to maintain.

Are we to understand that fidelity *creates* the indefectible?

Here we ought to reject categorically the idealistic interpretations. The role of fidelity consists not in creating anything at all, but in unrelentingly dissipating the clouds which threaten to overcast—what?—an image? Surely not, but a *presence* which images manifest or concretize in a very variable fashion. He who suffers from no longer seeing distinctly the one whom he mourns does not love any the less for that matter.

Will it be said that I am resuming the ontological argument in reducing it to naught? And on the other hand that I am taking as a point of support, not an idea, but an affective given? The truth is that my reflection is brought to bear on an experience in which the memory affects the character of piety. It is at the root of this experience that reflection discerns the presence of the indefectible, while at the same time it recognizes the unavoidably intermittent character of these manifestations.

I have been asked whether an experience of this kind has in my eyes a universal character. I am unable to come up with an answer. I can only utter and propose what my reflection comes up with in being brought to bear on my experience. Perhaps it is fitting to add that I find even within me the sceptic and the ungodly whom I cannot hope to convince entirely but only to disturb. This shows clearly enough that we are not concerned here with a demonstration of the immortal-

ity of the soul in the classical sense and that we cannot
even be concerned with anything of the kind.

It would be interesting to refer to my notes of yesterday which bear on the object, for example, on the
country house which no longer exists. In certain re-
spects it is obviously comparable to a body which is no
more than dust. But is there a sense in which this house
is a "soul" and survives? Without any doubt, will be
my answer, in as much as it has formed a center for a
certain *we* in which it is incorporated. It has contributed in founding an intimacy; but in return this intimacy raises it above the world of absolutely perishable
things and consecrates it. But this does not amount to
saying that it is thus assured the immutability of an
essence, but rather a life which is in some way measured
by the pulsations of memory.

Basically, in order to understand such a position, it is
a matter of exorcizing the notion of the object which
continues to exist even when there is nobody to perceive it.

Meanwhile one may counter my remarks and say: is
this indefectible presence in function of the act by
which it is called forth? My answer here is: surely not.
One could say that the relationship implied in the
image of sleep over which I keep watch tends to be
reversed, and that this presence in its turn can be
regarded as tutelary.

Passage to the I Exist

The affirmation of an *I am* is involved in the question which I am perpetually addressing to myself: Who
am I? Who is the "I" who questions me about what I
am ?

But to say "I exist" is to say "I am in the world," I
belong to a certain "concert," I am involved in a con-

sensus. I am told that I know that I have not always existed. Do I really know it? What does "to know" mean here? I must show that even this is obscure; but what is even more obscure, more uncertain, is the question of a future in which I will not have any part.

Le Peuch, August 4

The more I reflect on it the more it seems false to say: "I know that I have not always existed." There is here and there can only be a non-knowing. I do not know whether I participated in the world which preceded "my birth" and according to what modalities. It could moreover happen that, accidentally or not, I may one day obtain some light on this point. My very being partakes perhaps of this indefectibility in intermittence to which I have access when my fervor is centered on a deceased loved one. My birth or even what has preceded or followed it is only the object of hearsay knowledge. There is a sense in which I have the right to affirm that it is foreign to me.

When I say: "I am," I can simply paraphrase that to mean the assurance which bears on being. It would be formulated almost as precisely by saying: there is some being. We have here two slopes which come together at the summit.

I must try and grasp better in what consists the difference of the existential level (this is to be linked to what I said of the metaphysical import of human experience).

Perhaps we can here turn to account what I wrote on the everyday life. The everyday life pure and simple: it is the situation of a being who knows exactly where to find what he needs; the spoons and forks are in this drawer and for special occasions one can find the monogrammed silver in that other drawer. There we have an experience which can be presented sometimes as that of mastery, sometimes as that of subjection. I must consider the rapture of the discovery in contrast to this mastery-subjection.

The certitudes are comparable to resources that I have at my disposal. But these can depreciate in my eyes *precisely because I have them at my disposal.*

ESSENTIAL FUNCTION OF DISSATISFACTION

Notes on the Intermittent Indubitable

What seems interesting to me here is the effort to comprehend in a superior notion the eclipses of existential assurance, symbolized by the act which permits us to understand the necessary alternative of day and night. I ought to succeed in accounting for myself even when presence escapes me, that I do not for that matter have to doubt it, that it is no more really absent from me than the hidden sun. Absence should not be for me a motive for putting [presence] in question (just as during the night I do not doubt the existence of the sun; I know the reasons why I cannot see it all the time). Here we have something analogous *mutatis mutandis.* This means that I understand why it is essential to presence not to be always manifested, without my being able to say, however, that it is invariably my fault if it is eclipsed. Reality is much more complicated; and naturally there cannot be objectively formulable laws within the existential that permits me each time to account for these alternations and anticipating them. This is connected with the intersubjective character of presence.

Aside question but an important one: Can I at a

given moment discern my own existential level? At first sight it seems almost certain that I cannot do so.[1]

This level ought to correspond to the way in which is specified the personal affirmation of existence which underlies my experience at a given moment. But does this not depend on the way in which my fundamental attention is focused on that moment? Let us beware: what counts here is perhaps less the object on which the attention is centered than the perspective according to which the field of attention structures itself. This is still not clear enough; it will have to be made concrete. In the case of a book, for example, we must disinguish the different modalities which the interest for this book can affect. (It goes from curiosity to passion.)

Le Peuch, August 5

Yesterday evening it occurred to me that perhaps in setting out from the notions of availability, permeability and consecration we can better grasp what the existential level is. Perhaps someone will say: "These are only differences bearing on states." This supposes however that we take the word "state" in a very vague sense, more especially as in order to think of availability, one cannot eliminate the idea of a *"reference to,"* of a *"being attuned to."* Must we say that the difference in the existential level coincides with that of the closed and the open? It seems to me that we must go further and, as I pointed out yesterday, inquire how the affirmation *I exist* is specified. We must inquire also up

[1] Would not the truth be that I am at the same time on separate levels without my being always able to discern myself on which of these levels I am more myself. All expressions used in this matter are, moreover, unreliable. The chief difficulty arises from the fact that we can hardly rid ourselves of the spatial image of a core.

to what point it is legitimate to claim that the subject is not the same in the different cases. The best thing would undoubtedly be to say, not that it is not the same, but that it does not point to the same. But that is a term we still have to define precisely.

It would be best, after all, to refer to the earliest notes in which I took this distinction into account last March and April. I wrote on March 25: "What can count for me is an indubitable which cannot be put in question when I am at a certain level of my being. If it can never be put in question, then it is insignificant." Here is a precise illustration of what I wanted to say: there are moments in which I find a meaning to my life; it seems that I can then even accept the deceptions which have been the most cruel, that I can see why they had to be inflicted on me. There are other moments, however, when I am incapable of rising to this level, when I identify myself with the hurts and the deteriorations from which life has not spared me. In those moments I seem to have become the dupe of constructions built up by my imagination.

Another example is my way of appreciating my relatives, my nearest relatives. It may well be that I have as it were yielded to this or that immediate impression of friction, disregard or irritation. It can also happen on the contrary that I dissociate myself altogether from these immediate impressions and that I come to a much wider and purer appreciation of what they are in themselves and also for me. Cf. my notes of last May 3 and the letter to Berteloot in which I insisted on the fact of being centered on myself as on an ailing organ; that means in short self-complacency or self-pity (cf. *The Egoist* of Meredith).

Here, however, a possible confusion must be pointed out. One might be tempted to say that what matters is to arrive at objectivity. But this word is misleading. Objectively speaking it is doubtful that I can confer a meaning on my life. I think I was entirely justified in bringing value to bear on it. Everything I wrote on that subject at the end of my notes of May 3 last seems correct but is still insufficient: it is too negative. It is the link between existence and value that we must try to define. Note that value, more obviously even than presence, is intersubjective. Recently in the *Treatise on Morality* by Le Senne, I was looking over what he says concerning value. That satisfies me only partially. In a remarkable way he has been able to disclose the meeting point of something which comes from me, which is an aspiration, and something which is a gift and is as it were encountered. This is important; it frees us from the most devitalizing effects of idealism. But the very notion of value is not clear. I will see again in a little while what he says in *Obstacle and Value*.

While going through pages 175 and the following, I had the impression that they contain some important points. However, in spite of everything, the thought remains basically quite hazy. In his autographed dedication Le Senne wrote to me: *"It is value which gives existence to souls."* A beautiful formula and true, I think, but one that would also need to be more closely defined. I am always noting the difficulty of finding here some effective holds. I am convinced that I shall succeed in understanding the question of existence and that of value only simultaneously.

Today I am tempted to resume my initial notes of these last days (August 2). It would be necessary to inquire if I can conceive something indestructible. To the extent that the thought which raises this question is turned toward things, in as much as they can be labelled and inventoried, it seems certain that to this question there can be only a negative answer. The indestructible is here only the unformed, only what is below all destructions. If the endless deathroll that each of us is forced to compile for himself within so short an existence only illustrates imperfectly this affirmation which pertains to the object, it seems to remain certain that whatever is, is destined to perish. Consequently, whatever be the intrinsic value of the exigence of immortality that is in us and the metaphysical justification that it is capable of receiving, we must note that if it tries to translate itself into the world of objects, by the same token it condemns or refutes itself. This we see clearly; moreover, we are not in any way sure that it can be exempt from giving this disastrous translation of itself. But from this point of view the proof as such is annulled, or would be annulled, since failure is certain, unless it is reduced to a test of duration, which is absurd. We can understand nothing in human life if we do not grant that duration has nothing to do in the matter. Here value actually seems to intervene precisely as being independent of duration.

Value as a stake, or rather as a seal, of the existent. However, we have here so vague, so superficial and especially so equivocal a determination. Is value conferred from without? Surely not; it can only be recognized imperfectly. It is therefore primarily experienced. It seems to me that it can only be incarnated first in order to radiate later. This is important because such a manner of thinking frees us immediately from the psychological aspect. Nevertheless one might insist: incarnated for whom? This question is, however, suspect. In asking it, one seems to set up a radical duality between the one who incarnates and the other from whom he incarnates. But everything changes if we affirm in principle a certain unity of a *we*, a radical non-isolation of the subject, including even the primacy of the intersubjective. For, from this point of view it is no longer a question of affirming something which would be first incarnated purely and simply, and another subject which would later, as it were from the outside, become aware of this incarnation. This is clearer still if we understand that the intersubjective is really within the subject himself, that each one is for himself a "we," that he can be himself only in being many, and that value is possible only on this condition. But perhaps it is necessary to postulate in principle that this interior or intersubjective plurality maintains the closest and least easily explorable relations with the extra-subjective plurality. My own are not only represented in me, they are in me, they are part of my very being (double falsity of monadism: I am neither *alone,* nor *one*).

Le Peuch, August 6

The "we" reveals itself undoubtedly as really more profound than the "I." Despite appearances, it is certainly more stable (return of the Prodigal Son). What matters for me is the indestructibility of the "we." But this wish seems at first quite unreasonable. What is more fragile than the "we" if it is likened to an objective structure? Are not the quarrels, the ruptures, sufficient to show this? But it would be instructive to find out here how these quarrels and these ruptures come about, what they are due to. They are all explained by the pretentiousness of the "I" in affirming itself against the "we" (role of interests, of susceptibilities of prejudices and the like).

Would not the true existential movement always be the gaining of an access to a "we," or to an "ours," provided this "we" becomes a principle of intimacy and

not of constraint? Thus we would again come across
the availability concerning which I wrote this morning.
It goes without saying, moreover, that no one more
than the saint who prays in solitude has access to the
"we." To interpret sociologically what I said earlier
would be to distort my thought in a grotesque fashion.

The preceding remarks enable us to understand why
the indefectible cannot be present except in an intermittent way—perhaps because this inner "we" is itself
inevitably intermittent. I do not always communicate
with myself. To ask that it be there all the time is to
attempt to confer on it a mode of existence which is
that of the most rudimentary object, the nearest there
may be to non-existence. Here, however, a question
arises: can this intermittence be considered as an intrinsic characteristic of existence at its peak?

I believe that this question rests on a confusion very
similar to what I have denounced a little further back.
Existence in its higher forms is inseparable from intersubjectivity. That means that we cannot—and we neither can nor ought to *wish*—to raise ourselves somehow
above the intersubjective in order to think of presence,
for in fact we risk falling beneath it.

I seem to have made perceptible progress today.
However, I would like to try and reply more directly to
the questions raised yesterday and to define what I
called the existential pointer.

When I ask if I exist, I can imply the question: Does
something exist?

I can ask, in terms of a supposedly absolute existence
(God), if I myself exist.

But I can also ask what I mean when I affirm that I
exist or when I put the question to myself.

My awareness of existing can be presented in such a
diffuse way that it is really less that of my own existing

than that of existing in general (vegetative states). Only reflection can in some way qualify this vague state which being a simple state, absolutely lacks the characteristics of an affirmation. A certain existence being given or conceived, only reflection can lead me to inquire if my existence belongs to the same order, to the same degree, if I can exist more or less. Certainly a very belated distinction, one that will never be completely accepted since there is something in us which cannot admit of an intermediary between existence and non-existence. If, for instance, I am aware of my ephemeral character, shall I conclude from this that I exist less than a being that endures for a length of time? Not necessarily. Perhaps I shall say that in so far as I exist I do so absolutely. However my existence appears to me as something undermined or consumed by something which destroys it, which is another way of saying I do not exist purely and simply. Here we would therefore have the contrast between a pure and an impure existence. It remains to be seen if there is any basis for this contrast. Pure existence is not and cannot be given; consequently, neither is the impure existence any more given, in the sense in which I have just indicated.

It will be important to note that there is no reason for an existential philosophy to gravitate around anguish. I have in mind the intoxication of discovering, of exploring (a country, a musical score), which is perhaps the purest joy that I have ever experienced.

It is evident that the idea of a pure existing cannot find any guarantee in experience. It remains to be seen if an argumentation like that of Saint Thomas, who claims to go from finite to absolute existence, is admissible.

But it would be necessary to begin by recognizing, more distinctly perhaps than Saint Thomas has done, what we mean when we speak of existence, of this or that existent. I have the impression today of being still surrounded by a dense fog.

Nevertheless, I take up question formulated on the 2nd. What is the relation between existence and belonging to the world? The being who most belongs to the world is in a certain sense the most fragile; but he is also the most endowed with resources. Perhaps he is the one whose fragility is the most *compensated*. Perhaps we could thus conceive a being who would be at once susceptible to many hurts, but at the same time and for that very reason endowed with an infinite power of recuperation. This dual characteristic is already manifest in man, or at least he presents as it were an outline of it.

Le Peuch, August 7, 1943

I do not think that we can make much use of this last remark, at least not directly. On the other hand, I do not think it necessary to make any allowance for what I said concerning pure or impure existence. By imagining here the possibility of a *mixis*, I convert existence into an *essential* determination. The notes of August 2 on the other hand seem to retain their interest. However, a difficulty prevails: to exist, I said, is to make oneself stand out; but to make onself stand out is to make oneself stand out in reference to. Now, can we say that when we imagine existence we somehow picture it as dependent on the one who acknowledges it? But we must first ask ourselves once more if we really conceive existence—which converts it into an essential determination—and on the other hand if we do not conceive it how can we speak of it? There lies the central difficulty, the kind of perplexity around which one does not cease to turn. Here, as often, it seems that it is necessary to work out a distinction between some kind of initial experience which is to be restored in its candor and the sterotyped and more and more devaluated expressions of this same experience. At the root of existence there is first the recognition of a "Here I am!"—*exclamation as the soul of the existential*; transition to this idea that the child is actually more deeply involved than the adult in existence as such. But this "Here I am!" is treated as the manifestation of a "for itself," and the latter can be almost completely blinded. The "for itself" can be understood only as participation: to exist is to co-exist.

I refer to the phrase above concerning exclamation; it is equivocal. All that I would have the right to say is that exclamation is the soul of what I call perhaps improperly the judgment of existence. I would not mind saying that the existent is *the exclamatory grown cold* (the non-existent too, but in one case there is exclamation in presence of what is felt as fullness, in the other, of presence that is felt as emptiness). It may be objected that I tend to disregard the *intending*, the intentionality. But the latter is at the heart of exclamation. Intentionality implies as it were the affirmation of a "thou also." That is what I translated above by the word co-participation, one could also say co-implication.

My reference to the child is, I believe, very opportune: "Mother, look at this little bird or this little flower." The need to show, to call to witness, is here fully manifest in order as it were to give more volume, weight, *echo* to the initial experience. The contemplative will no longer have need of this attestation coming from the other; he finds in himself the echo which he needs.

I feel that these last remarks have a true bearing, but I do not succeed at this moment in disengaging this bearing completely.

If I am not mistaken, we can say that the thing procures from us—from a certain depth of our being which little by little will be covered over or sealed up by experience—the act by which we proclaim its existence. The need for naming is closely linked with this act: to know how it is called. Doubtless one can have pleasure in oneself giving it a name; but this pleasure is fought off by a kind of scruple, save where one knows truly that one has made a *discovery*; in this case I shall readily say that to name is in some way to baptize and even to recreate. Existence as we commonly conceive it or think we conceive it, is in some way dross or dregs in reference to this *discovered* existence. Here we again come across what I noted yesterday morning above the Chastang on the rapture of exploration. There is a radical difference between this rapture and the joy of understanding and explaining which can come only afterwards (like that of grasping the topography of a country which one has first circled at random; in this case something is lost and destroyed as when one begins to draw a map).

The character of existence will therefore be to discover itself, to reveal to itself (that is what the word "discrimination" inadequately indicated).

Value is inherent in what discloses itself. But this is so little *for me* in the exclusive sense that I feel the need to call to witness, or perhaps in certain instances to keep the secret but on condition that the others know the existence of this secret; then I intrigue them. A different case: I have discovered a being with whom I can directly enter into communication. Then the secret can be kept completely without losing its value. I wonder if in the case of the thing the calling to witness **is** not destined to make up for the imperfection of the bond which is established between the one who discovers and the thing discovered.

In that way is explained the importance, on the affective and personal level, of the question: does that exist? Reference to a possible exploration—fascinating. What does not exist has no interest at all; it cannot make the heart throb.

I must indicate as strongly as possible the fact that there is something passionately non-subjective in this discovery: the thing discloses itself to me, but this does not hinder the possibility of an accent of pride, arrogance, domination from being put on this "to me." It is to me and not to you that this thing disclosed itself (perhaps thanks to my perseverance, my audicity, my astuteness; all that is only mediatory).

Discovery fundamentally differs from what happens in invention; that is what lies at the root of the idealist conception.

But from this point of view, what no longer exists is what no longer responds to me.

Can one perhaps say that existence even thus conceived has a value? I hesitate to say yes. We will have to come back to it.

More and more I have the feeling of having made a discovery there. It is the phenomenological aspect of existence that is brought out into full light. The attitude of the subject cannot in any way be dissociated from the fact that something is revealed to him.

One could speak of an existential radiance. But what complicates everything is that I have to grow familiar with what has first revealed itself to me. This becoming habituated to a thing confers on it its value as object. From then on it begins to appear in a particular category of experience until the moment when I am obliged to cross it out because there is no longer any need to take it into consideration. But from the moment the thing is thus incorporated or categorized the initial existential radiance is dimmed. (Could we not say that value resides in the endurance of the existential radiance, or else is the latter itself the sign of the value?)

It is very interesting to observe that from this point of view the idea of pure existence takes on a positive meaning. It is that to which it is impossible to become habituated; it is what transcends all possible categorization. Yet it is necessary to remark that we can always, alas, employ words, however lofty be their theological or metaphysical bearing, without paying attention to what they mean. Consequently, we can be so dulled to the finer points of creation as to be no longer capable of marvelling at anything whatever. We have there a simple analogy: in one case we no longer think anything, in the other we no longer see anything.

Now I would like to relate all this more directly to what I wrote on August 2.

I was going to write, I believe I wrote before: the characteristic of existence is to be *greeted* from the outset, but what is greeted is not existence; it is the existent in so far as *revealing itself*.

Le Peuch, August 8, 1943

Without doubt, I should have indicated more clearly that the exclamation in question is essentially an admiration. It must be added that that which is revealed to me and which elicits from me a cry of admiration always has a form, let us say more precisely, an individuality. The latter, however, can be evanescent like the flowery design in a display of fireworks.

What I fail to see very clearly at this moment is the connection between all this and what I said previously of existence as resistance to the forces of destruction. Is this resistance inherent in the existence as such, or in the existent?

Le Peuch, August 9, 1943

I have wondered if I should not entitle the work intended for Jean Grenier and for which these notes are preparatory "The Existential Premises of Immortality."

It seems to me that it should focus my reflections on the act by which I affirm the existence of the being I have known or loved. What matters here is the loving kindness for the person who has been associated with my life—this being who is no longer there and who yet remains present to me. In what sense? What is this presence?

He is no more. This means "that he is no longer of this world." At the very most I would be able to know where his remains lie; but this information, whether I possess it or not presents itself to me as totally indifferent with regard to the essential (irrelevant). Is it necessary to say that in these circumstances what remains in me is the memory of an apparition which has vanished? An apparition which was connected with this thing thrown on the scrap heap, like the refrain which still haunts me was connected with this broken music box that I happened to stumble upon in some storeroom. Can I not think that, just as this refrain has survived in me whom it haunts and who whistles it, this apparition continues to haunt me?

It is of the utmost importance to note on the one hand that this comparison is *possible*, but at the same time all the piety in me rejects it. It is the essence of this piety I have now to define or at least to distinguish. From an objective point of view it is only superimposed like a kind of dressing to a factual situation which it would not be able to modify in itself. But it is precisely the validity of this objective appreciation that it is a question of examining. How does it come about that I have the awareness of betraying in some way the one who is no longer there—as one takes unfair advantage for example of an absence or a failing—by considering him thus? "It seems to me sometimes that death is like a great weakness," says Raymond Chavière, I think, in the *Lantern*. What would such an infringement be? What exactly would be infringed? It cannot be an order emanating from the other who by supposition no longer exists; nor, it seems, would it be an order emanating from myself purely and simply, for one does not understand what it could have of the sacred. But it is an order emanating from a "we" which lives on in me. One could still say that a portion of myself is in some way assigned or consecrated to the one who is no longer there in person. It is this consecrated "I" which rises up against what presents itself to me as a sacrilege. It is here that my reflections of August 3 would have to be brought in. But a deeper study of the matter still seems to be called for.

While writing these lines, and immediately after having written them, I was seized by an unbearable feeling of lassitude and emptiness. W*hat pretentiousness* in this persistently renewed quest! Why not recognize that this sustained presence is only the prolongation in the imagination of an experience actually consummated, completed? In the realm of imaginary or the unverifiable: does that not amount to the same? I have said everything in the final scene of *The Iconoclast*. I have never gone farther.

Feeling of dereliction.

But then how was I able to speak of an indefectible? Of course, while speaking of eclipse, it was precisely moments like this that I intended. But how can I during the eclipse continue to feel the strength and the right to affirm the eclipsed reality?

The word "pretentiousness" is essential. From the moment that *I make bold to establish*, I expose myself, as it were to a just punishment, to having to go through a phase of total discouragement afterwards. It is even *just*, I would say, that it be so. But in these conditions how is one to dare to think? After all it is actually I who thinks, who reflects.

Le Peuch, August 10, 1943

I return to my notes of August 2 by stating more precisely: If I consider the real usage of words, I observe that the stress is placed on the word "to exist" only when I say: Such a thing or such a person still exists or exists no longer, or in the case where to exist means to have a value. This stress disappears or is considerably weakened when I say: a country exists, or there are people who. . . . To exist is equivalent to standing out only in the first two instances. To exist certainly does not mean to sparkle; and yet it is legitimate to speak here of existential radiance as I have done. These sparks die down wherever existence is put in question.

One would observe very similar inqualities of stress by concentrating on the word "existence." It can simply mean a way of passing one's life: a full existence. On the other hand when one says : *it is not an existence* to live in such conditions, one implicitly indicates that a definite value is implied in existence.

On a strictly philosophical plane, to ask about the existence of the external world is to wonder if it has an existence of its own; perhaps one could state it more precisely and say an existence for oneself and not simply that of a spectacle for me the spectator. It is quite certain that the spectacle has an existence even as a spectacle; but this existence appears as precarious and derived. There would be no sense in asking ourselves whether things exist unless we were furnished with a previous existential assurance bearing on ourselves or on God. In fact it is the consciousness which thinks itself most lacking in this assurance that puts this question to itself.

It would be necessary to bring into focus what I wrote on pretentiousness, on the "I *make bold to establish.*" Why is this pretentiousness so shocking precisely where it is a question of existence? This pretentiousness is not shocking at all where what is in question is a certain objective sequence or a certain objective characterization. (I undertake to lead you to such a place; if need be, someone else too could just as well lead you to it.)

Does the existential in its full meaning disclose itself only to the subject? Does it merge then with the unverifiable? What I said earlier about intermittence is here revealing. A revelation is not reproduced at will. This is true in every domain. In hearing again such a musical work which at first upset me I am not sure of regaining my initial emotion.

One could sum up by saying that it is scandalous on my part to put forward a claim where I have been the beneficiary of a gift, a grace. But if existence is such as I have conceived it, then that is really the case here (cf. the notes of August 7).

Le Peuch, August 11, 1943

Perhaps it would be fitting to insist here on the link between existence and gift. All existence is perhaps in the precise sense of the word, let us not say given but offered. (Commonplace expression: a spectacle which is offered me.) We come across here the opposition that I pointed out some days ago between the point of view of invention and construction and that of discovery. It is probably the idea that a gift is intended for some person in particular that gives rise here to some confusion; whereas here it seems to be a question of an offering in the indeterminate (offering to one who will be able to profit from it).

Le Peuch, August 13, 1943

I did not jot down any notes yesterday.

This morning I thought that I might proceed to a sort of classification: the problem of existence does not at all arise in the same terms for:

things
persons
values
the world
God

It is with regard to things that it is raised the least, if one may say so, in the sense that we do not and cannot seriously doubt their existence. But it is also with regard to them that we least know what it can be to exist. Their existence is offered or proposed to us; but is it only the existence of a spectacle? No, since it offers us resistance.

Beings as such, as interiorities, can only be to be recognized and loved, for as masters who must be obeyed or as instruments to be utilized, they are not properly speaking beings.

On the other hand, contrary to those who invoke reasoning by analogy in order to account for the belief in the existence of others, I must say that I do not constitute myself as interiority except in so far as I take congnizance of the reality of the others.

Once the existence of things is posited as irrefutable, nay as the prototype of existence, what are we to say of the existence of beings? On the one hand, I can act as if I denied it; on the other, I can deploy in the service of this negation the resources of an idealist sophistry. This would be still more true with respect to God. I can act as an atheist. I am thinking at this moment of the hero of *Bel-Ami* which I have just reread. One cannot imagine a more radical atheist, whatever the opinions of the character may be; and one will always have the possibility of theoretically justifying this practical atheism.

Le Peuch, August 14, 1943

I thought this morning that worship seems necessarily to have to be reduced for the one who considers it from the outside to an activity which consists in maintaining and renovating images; in short to a commemoration. Communion has a radically unintelligible character for one who is not a communicant.

I wonder if the distinction between personal and impersonal *existence* would not provide a fairly good point of departure. "It exists," is said with respect to something for which one intends to propose a definition or a beginning of a definition: a country exists in which. . . . The stress is not laid on the uniqueness; it is rather the opposite. On the contrary, existence in the personal sense implies ipseity, reference to the lived actuality, included in the two contraries "still" and "no longer." A certain light still shines, or on the contrary it has been dimmed. From this point of view it seems that in fact I bestow existence only on that of which one can say: that still exists, or no longer exists, and this would radically exclude values, mathematical essences, etc.

I went to meet J. who came from La Roche and I read to her the notes on the indefectible. She thinks that they are good, but I am hesitant. Is it not by attachment to memory that I keep alive the images? It seems however that one can make this claim only by giving to memory a sort of ontological value, and then one comes back precisely to my position. At the root of the commemoration there lies an affirmation which most of the time does not in any way reach articulation; it is articulated even less in proportion as the commemoration is addressed to an indeterminate, like "the dead of World War I." It is far less true in a small village like this where he calls to mind some definite beings whom most people have known individually.

What is strange is that one admits so readily that the veneration of the dead is only a religion of memory, or, if one prefers, that it has as its point of application the *no longer existing*, that is to say, if one does not admit my position—the inexistent.

Le Peuch, August 15, 1943

I feel very strongly that what I have written on the metaphysical foundation of commemoration is not thoroughly worked out. All that has been loosely thought out.

At this moment I observe that I cannot think of one of the beings whom I have known and who are no longer of this world without a general emotion being awakened, as though there were canals which come together in a central reservoir. And I have come to the point of wondering if this emotion would not quite naturally be linked to the thought of the completion of my life so much of which is already spent. We would again come across this self-pity to which I am so inclined and which at the same time seems to me so suspect. However, in all good faith, this would be to distort what I feel. It is this presence-absence of the other that is for me an ever bleeding wound: if it were my obsession with the portion of life that is passed, why should it disguise itself in that way?

Well no, what I have written there is definitely not correct. What I cannot bear is the idea that they (Edith, little Ménès and so many others) have been treacherously taken by life. I must ask myself: What does it mean to be treacherously taken by life? I do not have the right to affirm that is not, that this cannot be the case. But from where do I get this right, on what is it based? That is the vital question that is at the heart of my obsession.

While on my way to the station just now, the idea has occurred to me that perhaps their presence is indicated in the way in which they help us to evoke them and to see them in another light.

It also occurred to me that men have become habituated these days to live in a world in which metaphysical injustice would triumph, in which one would truly be treacherously taken, and to incarnate in their life this supposed injustice.

Le Peuch, August 16, 1943

If I were certain that they are at peace and in the light, I do not say that my nostalgia would disappear, but it would lose its "consuming" character.

To be treacherously taken, what does that mean? There are beings who all their life have been magnetized by a diffused hope. We cannot bear the idea that they have been simply led to a position which would have horrified them if they had been knowingly lured into it. *Yes, led.* It is really a matter of finding out if this word has a meaning. One can attribute to it a meaning only where it is possible to have in mind a will or a power akin to a will. But are we obliged—or simply do we have the right—to think the series of events which form the framework of an individual life as being willed by some one or some thing?

The course I must follow is to distinguish several cases. If I have to consider my own self as willed, as called to being by a spiritual power, can I think that what happens to me is not in itself willed? But am I compelled to consider myself as willed? On the other hand, is it possible that I am there by chance? This is the question that governs all the others. It is connected with the problem of individuation and of its foundation.

Le Peuch, August 19, 1943

Under what conditions can I consider myself as willed? Could a character in a novel happen to conceive himself as willed by the novelist who has invented it? This question is absurd, precisely because the character is only a character. The question cannot arise for me except in so far as I am myself something else and something more than a simple character. The latter—the character in the novel—is "for itself," but it is a "for itself represented," "for itself for the other," if one may say so. The character cannot cut itself off from this system of perspective in which it is so to say enclosed, except on condition of being denied as a character and of being changed or reabsorbed into the novelist himself, as is the case in certain contemporary works: *The Counterfeiters, Point Counterpoint,* etc.

Le Peuch, August 20, 1943

It is perfectly clear that when I tell myself that I am willed by God, I do not know what this *I* means. Does it refer to the one that I am *here and now?* But this one has no independent existence at all. Does it refer to what I ought to become? But what does the word "ought" mean here? Is it an "I should?" or an "I am destined to?" This indeterminateness suffices to render the meaning of the question so obscure that one does not know how one could reply to it.

This evening, I had a long metaphysical and theological conversation with J. What confusion in my thoughts! What uncertainties! I am too much aware of difficulties at times; I no longer see clearly. It is absolutely necessary to take up again the immortality-eternity question. The solution of Father Laberthonnière, although it conforms to quite a long tradition, seems to me confused and ambiguous. He is too afraid of appearing to justify the criticisms and sarcasms of Brunschvicg.

Le Peuch, August 22, 1943

Etienne Borne has asked me to send him some notes on Evil. I had better begin with the question put on June 26, 1942: What do we expect in fact, and what can we expect in principle, from a philosophical theory of evil? Can it be in the precise sense of the term an explanatory theory? We are dealing with the presence of evil within reality. The theory can be explanatory

only if evil is considered as a flaw in a kind of function-
ing.
It could concern:

 a) either a functioning of "things" themselves;
 b) or a functioning of thought which bears on
things, thought here being itself more or less
similar to a sense like vision or hearing, a
sense subject to disorders that are clearly defin-
able but not necessarily curable. An oculist can
tell someone: your vision is faulty because
your retina is ill, without guaranteeing that he
will find the means for curing this retina.

The distinction between a) and b) is important, at
least at first blush. In one case, in the world such as it is
constituted, I spot the existence either of a defect or of
a disturbing cause. In the other case I say: the world as
it is cannot incur any reproach, but the same does not
hold good for the knowledge of which it is the object.
Let us be on our guard, however; knowledge is here
likened to an instrument which would be distinct from
the spectacle on which it bears. But it is a question of
ascertaining if it is not simply meaningless to treat
knowledge in this way. Indeed, [I must choose] one of
two things: either by the world I mean a spectacle; in
this case the question of good or of evil doubtless
cannot even be raised. For a pure spectator, supposing
that these words make any sense, there is neither good
nor evil. Or else, I understand by the world something
more than a pure spectacle, and in this case the distinction between spectacle and spectator must be changed.
If I am not before the world as a spectator confronting
a spectacle, it is because I participate in the world in
some way. This is also the reason why every imperfection in me is in some way an imperfection of the world

itself. It follows from this that case b) is actually reduced to case a). It remains to be seen, however, if in
these conditions there can still be a question of explanation in the strict sense of this word. An explanatory
thought can only set itself up as exempt from the
defects for which it intends to account. It is in the
name of a definite order which it conceives and with
which it identifies itself that it is capable of conceiving
the disorder and of recognizing in what it consists. This
is completely obvious within the nosological domain.
Can evil be compared to a sickness of reality? This
would suppose that it is possible for thought to conceive a healthy world. But this is not saying enough and
the word "to conceive" could mislead us. The science
of nosography in all its aspects is possible only on the
basis of an experience bearing on the organism in its
normal condition. But in our case the idea of a similar
experience is absurd. What takes its place is exclusively
an aspiration, an exigence, of which we do not know if
it can be effectively satisfied, nor even very precisely to
what it tends. In other words, to the being as it ought
to be we oppose the being as it is. But there is strict
opposition only for one's conscience. I know or I feel
that I ought to act in such a way, and yet I am unable
to refrain from acting otherwise. In this privileged instance, can there be explanation in the sense specified
above? That seems very doubtful. Anyhow, we would
have to go into the matter more deeply. In the final
analysis the problem bears less on what I do than on
what I am. To say, "I should act differently," is it not
basically to say, "I should be different from what I
am"? But does this make any sense? Perhaps, if by that
I affirm in a confused manner that in my innermost
being I am not such as I reveal myself. It is therefore

necessary that this "I should be" rests on an "I am." Otherwise we are in the realm of the unreal, perhaps in even that of mere words. This should be delved into thoroughly.

Le Peuch, August 23, 1943

Yesterday evening there came to me an idea which is not perhaps something to be kept but which I would like to try to elucidate. Evil can perhaps find no place in the world considered as ground, that is to say as the field of action or of play common to all, or again as the place of an objective thought. As a result all nosography of the real would be absurd. It could appear only within the perspective of a subject as subject, within my universe in as much as it is mine; or more precisely, the evil would always be a blow felt from my point of view as subject, something like an injury. Moreover, this would not in any way imply the ideality of evil, for it could happen that this very perspective would be more real than that of a depersonalizing and depersonalized thought.

I have not expressed this to my satisfaction and I am still not in a position to see if there exists here a paradox, a truism or an absurdity. It would be necessary to illustrate the matter by taking as example this or that iniquity, this or that act of cruelty, of which I myself have not been the victim but to which I do not react less intensely than if I had suffered directly from it. Certainly I affirm that there is evil there, an expression of evil in the most real sense. It remains to be seen if this real evil can be compared to a malformation, to a structural defect or a defective functioning capable of being detected or located. I do not succeed in recapturing my insight of yesterday evening. I should recall it as it came to me[1]—therefore I should go further back and especially inquire about what I wrote yesterday toward the end and which appears to me equally doubtful.

"To say: 'I should act differently,' is to say: 'I should be different from what I am,'" I noted yesterday and this seems to me correct. But what follows is doubtful. What sense is there in saying, "I should be different from what I am"? It is obvious that this does not make sense except within rather narrow limits. It would be absurd to say that I should be a girl even if I was convinced that this would be a blessing for my family —or that I should to be intelligent, and the like. There is in short a lower limit to my nature which I must take as given. Being as I am, having for example definite intellectual powers, I should be a worker. But is that not simply tantamount to "I should act differently"? Perhaps not. The meaning is: having such and such a quality, I should also have that other quality; but this other quality is not simply lacking in me like a gift that was refused to me. That is where, in this precise articulation, responsibility would enter the picture; but at the same time I would always have the means to deny responsibility by treating the deficient quality as a refused gift. By treating as a simple statement of fact what is at bottom a refusal, I definitely distort it.

We should now see how this remark can affect the philosophy of evil. I explain why I do not work: I am too preoccupied, or else the weather is too beautiful,

[1] I simply meant that any explanatory theory is developed according to a perspective in which precisely evil cannot be grasped as evil. Consequently it makes its object disappear from the moment it unfolds. The explanatory thought, which is by its very nature depersonalizing, cannot respond to an experience with which it has nothing in common.

and the like. But I mention these reasons in order to dispense myself from willing. The explanation appears like an alibi of the will. Here occurs the misunderstanding which I denounced in the note above. I recognize the evil which is in me only from the moment I renounce explaining, arguing. Is this applicable to the evil which is located outside me? But it would be necessary to begin by asking if localization here is feasible. Someone recounts to me an act of cruelty which has been committed thousands of miles away. I do not hesitate to declare that the evil, which I denounce along with the narrator, is localized in its perpetrator. But what are we to think of this characterization? My judgment can legitimately bear only on the act itself: but the one who has done it can have acted in complete and provoked ignorance. Here localization and accusation coincide and merge.

A supplement to my notes of yesterday. It is evident that a particular evil can involve an explanation and be compared to a malfunctioning. It is for the evil in its totality that the argument elaborated yesterday comes into play. On the other hand, note that beneath the explanation one proceeds already to a manipulation when one speaks of evil as of a principle which would have an intrinsic unity.

Le Peuch, August 25, 1943

To illustrate what I wrote in yesterday's supplement.

Someone informs me of the premature death of a being who was loved by his family and was marvelously gifted. If I refrain from offering some edifying cliches against this reality, I acknowledge that his death is an evil, everyone is indeed frustrated by it. This event taken in itself, in what I would today call its facticity, admits of some explanations: An illness of which perhaps one can discern the causes. The explicable here is found together with the inexplicable. The inexplicable is that the real implies the possibility of a determinism which works to the detriment of value. (I am here using a language that does not satisfy me fully.) Can I explain to myself the existence of this flaw in reality through which such a determinism is introduced? Can I compare it with a defect of construction in a machine? But we must go beyond this. Can I entertain the idea of an intact world similar to that of a normally functioning machine? I note that in the example of the machine two cases are to be distinguished. The one is the case of some specimen which is defective in relation to a definite type which would not be defective. The other is the case where the type itself shows some imperfections. Evidently the first case must be left aside, since the world cannot be compared to one specimen among others. Let us therefore examine the second. On what does the imperfection of the type bear? The machine is intended to render some service, to supply some product, and the noted imperfection diminishes this performance. Therefore, by starting with the idea of the end realized, we would have to find the means of avoiding the defect in question. Undoubtedly the judgment does in no way allow itself to be separated here from the exercise of a technician's thought, even if one cannot strictly say that it is this technician's or manufacturer's thought which carries the judgment. (I note in 1959 that this should be taken up again within the perspective of cybernetics.)

But precisely in an example like the one from which I started off in my note of today, nothing can be imagined which involves the exercise of a similar thought. Whereas I know perfectly why and for what purpose the machine is there, there is no sense in saying: why has the being whose loss I mourn appeared? And I can in no way determine the conditions which have rendered his appearance possible.

Le Peuch, August 26, 1943

What I wrote yesterday seems to me very poor. Phenomenologically I do not see that we are inclined to imagine what we call reality as an imperfect machine. The existence of a loved one does not present itself to us like an effect resulting from a particular way of functioning. Our imagination is rather dualistic and tends to represent reality as indifferent or hostile toward this being that appeared, then disappeared.

Le Peuch, August 27, 1943

I think that I was wrong in choosing too particular an example. However, I believe, no other example is more significant than it. The real presents itself to us as the milieu where this being was born and grew up, and from which he derived the elements of his own reality. Can one conceive that this milieu wanted him, even in a confused way, or that it was on the contrary totally indifferent with respect to him? This question is extremely difficult to pose in clear terms. It does not, however, seem that we can attribute to a milieu anything that resembles a will, because it has in itself no unity in as much as it is simply a milieu.

Presence and Immortality
(1951)

Each of us can, at certain times, have the feeling that the world is set up in such a way as only to foment in us the temptation to despair. From the moment that this temptation makes its presence felt, incitements adapted to reinforce it seem to surge up on every side. That is what I meant when I previously wrote about being encompassed by despair. We should not reply that these are moments of lassitude or discouragement; sometimes alas! they manifest themselves as moments of the most merciless lucidity. In the moments I recall, I seem to have suddenly rejected or torn up the veil of comforting illusions which masked life for me and by means of which I strove to provide for myself an endurable existence. It is as if suddenly life presents to me the petrifying face of the Medusa; this fascinating power seems to press into its service my desire for rectitude, my desire not to let myself become deluded. This is the hour of tragic pessimism. Surely it can, if need be, emerge into a philosophy of heroism; but it can also lead either to suicide or to the surrender of a being who breaks down when pitted against a scandalous world.

It can be said on the whole that in my work I have undertaken to find out if it is possible to resist this fascination, to cut off the Medusa's head without falling back into a lie. In this sense I will readily say that, if the mythological hero-type for Sartre is Orestes, for me it seems to be Perseus. I say that in a general way and without stopping to ask what Andromeda is.

But it is important to state precisely what for me is the authentic character of despair. Here I do not intend to analyze it psychologically, but to inquire what essentially is despairing. Perhaps it is neither wholly a thought, nor wholly a representation. Despair is a hybrid, it is a thought which is in process of becoming a representation; or perhaps it is the other way around. Here the image of the succession of generations, together with the connected ideas of place and function, play a determining role.

As a concrete illustration of this I have only to recall the indescribable gloom which I see emanate from the offices of the notary public. This gloom is in my opinion worse than that of the cemeteries, perhaps because the accumulated dossiers strike us as a ridiculous and sham substitute for perenniality.

As far as I am concerned, these images may well have this particularly despairing value for me, only because they stimulate in me a person who has been traumatically shocked since childhood by the death of another person, by the disappearance of my mother. This happened when I was about to turn four. I do not hesitate to say that my whole life—and even that of my spirit —has developed under the mark of the death of other persons. There lies the remote origin of the controversy which was to bring me into conflict with Léon Brunschvicg, at the Descartes Conference in 1937. When he reproached me for attributing more importance to my own death than he would to his, I answered him without hesitation, "What matters is neither my death, nor yours; it is the death of the one we love." In other words, the problem, the only essential problem is posed by the conflict between love and death. If there is in me an unshakeable certitude, it is that a world deserted by love can only be swallowed up in death. But it is also true that, where love persists, where it triumphs over whatever tends to degrade it, death cannot but be definitively vanquished.

It is essentially in this perspective that the reflections on hope which I made sometime ago and which are in reality at the heart of my entire work, must be seen. It is indeed no coincidence that I developed this phenomenology of hope during the war, in a lecture given in Lyon, in Fourvière, in the early part of 1942 if I am not mistaken. Father de Lubac, whom I had visited a few months earlier, had asked me to come and deliver a lecture before the whole Scholasticate of Fourvière. I unhesitatingly replied: agreed, I shall speak on Hope. That surely meant above all hope of liberation. My thought turned first toward the innumerable prisoners in the German camps. But it goes without saying that I could not for one second disregard the metaphysical resonances of such a problem and I had to find the connection between the hope of liberation and hope in immortality.

This whole investigation could be articulated only by starting out from what came to me as a discovery—that of the difference, often ignored even by the most distinguished persons, between desire and hope.

Desire is by definition egocentric: it tends toward possession. The other is then considered only in reference to me, to the enjoyments which he can procure me if I am full of lust; or he is seen simply in relation to

the services which he will be able to render me. Hope
on the other hand is not egocentric: to hope, I have
written in *Homo Viator*, is always to hope for us. Let us
say that hope is never the state of wishful thinking
which can express itself by an "I would very much wish
that." Hope implies a prophetic assurance which is
really its armor and which prevents the being from
breaking down, internally first of all; but it also prevents him from giving up, that is to say from surrender-
ing or degrading himself. I cannot help but recall here
the admirable strains which Péguy discovered in order
to eulogize hope in the *Porche de la Deuxième vertu*.
But the role of the philosopher is to raise to the level of
articulated thought what is here only preknowledge and
song.

In the preface, published under the title *La Parole
est Aux Saints* which I wrote for Madeleine Deguy's
beautiful play, *The Condemned*, I have observed that
the fact that men are able to face death for an idea,
without a *personal* hope to sustain them, can alone
definitely place beyond dispute this vocation, this ordination to the absolute by which man transcends nature
and manifests his irreducible singularity. From this
standpoint, I added, could we not say that, if the
believer is ahead of the non-believer on the road of
knowledge and love, the non-believer would be able to
be ahead of his rival in the order of pure willing and of
risk? Moreover, it goes without saying that this opposition of believer and non-believer corresponds to a sche-
matic view which is not and cannot be entirely adequate for reality. The believer is never totally believing;
it is impossible that he may not know some hours of
uncertainty and anguish in which he rejoins the unbe-
liever; inversely the latter can be animated by a belief
that he carries within him, which sustains him, but

which he is incapable of bringing to full consciousness. The impossibility for each one of us to know exactly what he believes and what he lives off is a constant theme in my philosophical writings, as in my plays.

But in these conditions, the function of the philosopher consists in bringing to the light of reflection, by a new type of maieutic, the implications of the life of thought, or rather of the life of faith. The latter ordinarily remains in a state of semi-obscurity from which consciousness does not succeed in drawing us out. It is on purpose that I have made use of the term "maieutic"; it brings out very well the Socratic aspect of my thought on which I have placed emphasis in the foreword to the *Mystery of Being*.

One of my friends, a Russian philosopher, who to me seems strangely in tune with my thought and to whom I spoke of this new maieutic, said to me: "Yes, it is a child of eternity that it is a matter of bringing into the world." The expression which at first sight surprised me a little, appears to me on reflection to fit exactly what is alive in question. But what is this child of eternity? It is in the last analysis *the being* in me, who, though not fully attainable on earth, aims at freeing himself from the categories ascribed to having—categories of desire, of self-love, and of fear. But one will recognize easily how this is related to our topic when one sees that these categories are in the last analysis centered on my body. Those who are the least bit familiar with my *Metaphysical Journal* know that in the subsequent development of my thought since the end of the first world war, my body presented itself to me as the locus of having, this locus itself being characterized by an essential ambiguity, or if one prefers an inner tension. This applies to all having: what I possess in a certain sense forms part of me, and this is expressed by the wrench that I feel deeply, when what I possessed is taken away from me in some fashion. But in another sense, what I possess does not really form part of me, since I can lose it without ceasing to exist or to be myself. This contradiction is, however, only an all too simplified expression for a very complex vital situation, which these categories do not permit accounting for precisely. But, as I indicated, my relation to my body presents already to the utmost this singularity and this duality. On the one hand, I am inclined to treat my body as something that I possess, which I can dispose of in one way or another. On the other hand and in a more profound way my body rebels to being treated like that, and this rebellion expresses itself through this affirmation, which, though philosophically very obscure, is one which is like a protestation coming from the depth of myself: my body is not something that I have; *I am my body*. The meaning of that phrase can be elucidated only in a negative way. To say "I am my body" signifies above all, I am not in a position to define any type of a relation which would unite these two terms, my self on the one hand, my body on the other. For example, I cannot say: my body is my instrument, or rather: it can be convenient for me to represent it thus to myself. A deeper reflection shows me that in the last analysis this thought is false, for the notion of instrument sends me back to the body, since every instrument is a certain extension of the powers of the body. Consequently, if I treat these powers as instrumental, I engage myself in an infinite regression.

I am my body is in reality an affirmation-center, an affirmation-pivot which can only partially be clarified according to the different perspectives that I may have to adopt, but without any one of them being accepted exclusively or definitely. That is what I have in view when I speak of a mystery of incarnation in a sense which is completely free of theological implications.

Let us try now to establish a connection between these general views and the phenomonological analysis of survival:

One can affirm in principle, it seems, that the more the relationship which has united me to another being has been strictly possessive, the more his disappearance must come to be likened to the loss of an object. True, the lost object can under certain exceptional conditions be found again, but one cannot attribute to it any *presential* character. Moreover, we will presently have to examine more deeply what exactly presence means.

But the situation changes if, to revive an excellent distinction of the Genevan psychiatrist, Dr. Stocker, my love is not possessive but *oblative*. Let us pause a moment on this distinction. It will be fitting to say that possessive love is self-centered, whereas oblative love is other-directed. Moreover, one meets again here in some way the famous distinction of the Swedish theologian Nygren, between *eros* and *agapē*. But in my line of inquiry, perhaps it would be necessary to add: human love—and this word must be understood in a meaning broad enough to be applicable also to friendship, to *philia*—implies a reciprocity profound enough to let other-directedness work both ways, to let each become the center for the other. Thus is created a unity which is not less mysterious than that which I spoke of in relation to incarnation. Furthermore, it is in the articulation of these two mysteries that the mystery of generation is contained.

"But," one will ask, "is not the idea of presence dangerously ambigious? What is the presence in question? In entitling your text *Presence and Immortality*, you seem to envision a trans-subjective presence, a real presence of the being who is loved beyond death. But on the other hand by bringing in the distinction between possessive and oblative love, do you not remain in a realm within the consciousness of the subject? Perhaps what you succeed in showing is that the being whom I lost will remain interiorly present to me in a much more intimate way if I have vowed this oblative love to him, than if I loved him only for myself and in a possessive way. But is it possible to go farther and to pretend that this presence does not belong merely to the realm of the memory, that it is *real?*"

There, indeed, lies the crucial question the difficulty of which one should not underestimate.

It seems fitting to bring in here what I have called secondary reflection, that is to say to compel the one who formulates the objection to disengage the assumption that it implies. It consists in applying to the realm of presence categories relating to the world of perception and of objectivity. I intended to show that it is precisely these categories which we must renounce.

The Italian philosopher Pietro Prini, in the profound study that he has dedicated to my thought, has called it the methodology of the unverifiable. It is very true that as far back as my first writings—I am here alluding to unpublished texts of 1912 and 1913—my concern has been to define a positive and concrete unverifiable and to show that it was the source of love and faith. Today I would certainly hesitate to make use of the term "unverifiable." In my ideas at that time, this term "unverifiable" had for its counterpart a truth taken in the very narrow meaning given to this word in the natural sciences. But what has persisted throughout the changes which have taken place in the terminology is this idea that we have to overcome, in order to approach presence, the notion that we form for ourselves of any object and of its structural conditions.

"In order to disengage the difference in the spiritual quality which separates the object from presence, I have stated in the *Mystery of Being*, it is proper to take as a point of departure certain very simple and immediate experiences, but the philosopher up to our time has always had a tendency to neglect them. For instance, we can have a very strong feeling that someone who is there in the room, very close to us, someone whom we see and hear and whom we can touch, is nevertheless not present. He is infinitely farther from us than such a loved one who is thousands of miles away or who even no longer belongs to our world. What then is this presence which is here lacking? It would not be correct to say that we cannot communicate with this individual who is there very close to us, for he is neither deaf, nor blind, nor half-witted. Between us a certain material communication is assured, but only a material one. It is in every way comparable to the kind which can be set up between two distinct stations, one sending and the other receiving. However, the essential thing is lacking. One could say that this is a communication without communion, and that for this reason it is an unreal communication. The other hears the words that I say; but he does not hear me and I can be painfully aware that these words, as he relays them back to me, words which he reflects upon, become for me unrecognizable. By a singular phenomenon, the other thus interposes himself between me and my own reality; he makes me in some way a stranger to myself; I cease in some way to understand myself and finally I no longer adhere to my own words."

But, by an inverse phenomenon, it can happen on

the contrary that the other, if I feel him present, renews me interiorly in some way. This presence is in such a case revelatory: it makes me be more fully myself than I would be without it" (*loc. cit.*, Vol. I, p. 220–221). This experience that I have had a hundred times is one of the most mysterious that exists and it appears to me to be among those to which philosophers have never paid any attention. One could say that it is, in the best sense, existential. For it is not so much what the other says, the content of his words which exercises on me this stimulating action, but it is *he himself saying these words,* he himself inasmuch as he sustains his own words by all that he is. But it is necessary to add that these experiences manifest an essentially gratuitous quality. Of course, I do not take this word here in the depreciated significance that one hears given to it when for example one speaks of a gratuitous act. Here gratuitousness implies grace, that is to say, at least negatively something which is beyond any know-how, beyond any teachable technique. It would be obviously utopian to hope that one can teach a man the art of making himself present to the other. One can teach only gestures and grins. This art is truly a grace; and inversely not to possess it is a disgrace.

But to insist on the non-objective character of presence does not at all amount to saying that it is only subjective. Actually it is necessary to speak of intersubjectivity here. The meaning of this term, however, is always in danger of being misunderstood because the world of ordinary activity is that of objects, and therefore one is apt to interpret intersubjectivity as a transmission bearing on a content that is objective and independent of those who transmit it. But that would only be a distorting interpretation of something which in no way allows itself to be expressed in such a language. Intersubjectivity is essentially an openness. I have often said that the distinction between the open and the closed introduced by Bergson in *The Two Sources of Morality and Religion* has undoubtedly a greater importance than he suspected. It would be important to go deeper into it and to bring out its implications. It seems that they emerge only in a philosophy of light. I take this word in a meaning very much akin to that which is given to it in the Gospel according to St. John, while specifying, however, that in my present perspective it is not only possible but necessary, at first, to be on this side of Revelation properly so called. More precisely, it is possible and necessary to limit oneself to areas which in the light of theology seem undoubtedly to be illuminated by it, but without one being necessarily obliged to becoming explicitly conscious of the central core of this Revelation. One may very well, for example, speak of the light of knowledge. I will even say that one is bound to do so. Failing this, epistemology itself becomes dry and distorted. But to point to this light at a certain level of thought is not necessarily to go back to its source.

One could say that intersubjectivity is the fact of being together in light. Here, as always perhaps, by proceeding negatively one can approach the positive essence toward which it is a matter of directing one's thought. If, in the presence of another person I am burdened with mental reservations about him, or if, which amounts exactly to the same thing, I attribute to him some ulterior motives concerning me, it is obvious that we are not together in light. I put myself in the shade. At once, he ceases to be present to me, and reciprocally, I can no longer be present for him.

These remarks seem capable of clarifying what I wanted to say when I said that it is necessary to transcend the categories of objectivity, for example, those which come into play when a doctor examines a sick person. I am leaving aside the case of the psychiatrist which raises special difficulties.

However, we must not overlook the fact that the transition from such observations to the question which occupies us cannot be brought about easily. Here again a serious objection must be foreseen. "In the cases of which you have spoken," someone will say, "the feeling of presence and of non-presence is in spite of everything supported by a properly objective relation. The being who is present to me *is there*; he is objectively there: is it not arbitrary and even illegitimate to dare to perform a radical dissociation between presence and objectivity? Are we not justified in saying that since objectively the departed is no longer there—or, which comes to the same, is reduced to some dry bones or to a handful of cinders—this indispensable foundation is lacking, so that presence is reduced to a purely subjective feeling?"

But experience interrogated without prejudice shows us clearly that it is impossible to hold fast to such summary assertions or statements. A fact so rigorously established as telepathy suffices to show us that there exist modes of co-presence which are irreducible to the type of juxtaposition involved in our everyday dealings with other men. Those who have most seriously reflected on telepathy—for example I am thinking of Carrington, and also of Price—have recognized that such phenomena imply a kind of specific unity among beings.

But this is not all. A more profound reflection leads us to put in question the very link between presence and objectivity. It would be necessary to take into account other experiences which occur in dimensions very different from the spiritual life. I am think-

ing in particular of creation, and especially of dramatic
or musical creations. It suffices to recall the way in
which a melodic idea arises for example. It occurs to us,
takes hold of us; where does it come from? Does it
come from myself or from somewhere else? It pertains
to reflection to recognize that this distinction is devoid
of all meaning. It supposes in effect an illusory topography; for there is actually no sense in admitting that I
constitute a circumscribed territory, in asking myself
whether this idea originates within this territory or
not—as one would do for a stream which has its source
on this or the other side of a particular boundary. In
reality, the idea of an I-territory is a ficticious idea, and
one cannot make any appreciable correction in it by
introducing the notion of a subconscious which would
be like the underlying complement or the substructure
of this area. Idealism, at least in its subjective forms,
has unfortunately too often appealed to a myth of this
sort without which monadism cannot be established.
And I will add that the astonishing bad will which so
many philosophers, authentic or not, have shown toward metapsychical phenomena, stems from the fact
that they cling to this fiction and that these phenomena actually manifest this capital interest of compelling any one who considers them honestly to break
through his mental categories. Here is realized as it
were a merger between the metapsychical experience on
the one hand, and an autonomous reflection on the
other. Such a merger is calculated to put in question,
on the speculative level, the post-cartesian philosophy
in so far as it is centered on the *cogito* under its
restrictive form—whereas only the criticism of the *self*,
the *I* can open for us the doors of a liberating metaphysic.

Yet a delicate question arises here: what useful pur-

pose can metapsychical research serve with respect to
the question, let us say, not yet of immortality, but of
survival? From the same point of view that I have
adopted, this question becomes extremely acute, for if
one considers that experience can teach us something
about this matter, does one not risk re-establishing at
the same time a certain objectivity in the very domain
where one had wished to transcend it? It seems that my
answer would more or less take the following form.

First of all, I do not think that one can contest the
importance of those investigations for the problem of
survival. A certain number of precise facts hardly
admit an explanation without the hypothesis of an
entelechy which outlives what we call death. This hypothesis is all in all the simplest and the most economi-
cal. It is possible that one can hope to come upon a
beginning of verification. Nevertheless, it will be a question only of hypothesis. But, the presence which I am
thinking of is supra-hypothetical: it gives rise to an
invincible assurance which is connected with oblative
love. It expresses itself by some such affirmations as: "I
am assured that you are present to me and this assurance is linked with the fact that you do not stop
helping me, that you help me perhaps more directly
than you could on earth. We are together in the light.
More exactly, in moments when I am detached from
myself, when I cease to eclipse myself, I gain access to a
light which is *your* light. Surely I do not mean the light
of which you are the source, but that in which you
yourself blossom, that which you help to reflect or
radiate upon me.

I will add that for the being still not set free who I
am, this invincible assurance is reinforced *indirectly*
through facts which are evidences or more exactly
breaches: breaches in the prison in which I enclose

myself as soon as I hypnotize myself with what is objectively given. I said "reinforced," I did not say "grounded." Here, as elsewhere, we stumble upon the ambiguity of our condition which is that of a being who is involved in the world of things and in which he participates, but on the other hand, transcends this world and knows that he transcends it. Moreover, we again encounter here the articulation of freedom and grace which, in a thought like mine, presents itself as the pivot of spiritual activity. This world of ours is so structured that I can find around me every reason for despairing, for seeing in death the annihilation and the miserable keyword of the incomprehensible existence into which I have been senselessly thrown. But to a deeper reflection, this world appears simultaneously as being so constituted that I can become conscious in it of the power I retain to withstand these appearances, to deny to death this ultimate reality. Therein lies, moreover, the meaning of the word "unverifiable" to which I have had recourse. The reality or scope of death is not independent of the way in which I judge it; rather it would be necessary to say in which I gauge it. But I will add, while staying always on this side of Revelation and the promises of Scripture, that metaphysical reflection, and to some extent metapsychical experience permit me to select signs capable of conferring on this free act a minimum guarantee which I need. I need this guarantee because despite everything I continue to remain the center of a critical and polemic reflection, which, if it does not overcome itself, is secretly attracted by despair and nothingness. These signs have a consistency just sufficient for doing their job; if they were proofs, my freedom before death would be as it were annulled and so, as happens among certain naive spiritists, life as well as death would find itself stripped of its seriousness, the sacrifice shorn of its tragic and ultimate grandeur. We meet here the theme admirably developed by Peter Wust, the metaphysical value of risk as condition of the human existence attained in its mysteriously specific character.

Besides, it is proper to go farther and to observe that as the idea of immortality infinitely transcends that of survival, it is impossible not to go into theology properly so called, that is to say, not to go back to the very source of all light, to God and to His love for creatures. Thereby one is actually committed well beyond a philosophy of presence properly so called, and it becomes impossible to not appeal to the dogma illustrated by the revelations of the saints. But here I have deliberately remained on this side of a fence which the philosopher as such can cross over only with difficulty.

Truly speaking, I am sure that some people will protest against such an attempt as I am making here and will contest the value and the cogency of a thought which strives beyond objectivity to present some concrete approaches to Revelation. Let me declare categorically that the image of a bridge, if it should unavoidably suggest itself to the mind, must be rejected, since it cannot be a question for philosophical thought properly so called to infringe in any way upon the domain of Revelation. However, I persist in thinking that it is important to show how reflection, wherever it is deployed in all its dimensions and becomes recuperative, proceeds by an irresistible movement to encounter an assertion which transcends it, but in the end enlightens it with respect to itself and to its proper nature.

The Unfathomable

An Unfinished Play

(March, 1919)

CHARACTERS

Robert Lechevallier
Gustave Lechevallier
Father Séveilhac
Edith Lechevallier, *Robert's wife*
Georgette Lechevallier
Mrs. Lechevallier
Lise Breton
Francine Vadot

At the Lechevallier home. A gloomy living-room in a rather dismal apartment in the neighbourhood on rue du Bac in Paris. The action takes place in the Spring of 1919.

SCENE ONE

EDITH, GEORGETTE, *both knitting*

GEORGETTE—In brief, you have found him changed after all?

EDITH—*after a moment*—No. His face is a little thin; that's all.

GEORGETTE—Yes, that is also how he appeared to me. But before the war I knew him so little! Remember he came just for our wedding. Moreover, there are memories on which one can no longer rely.

EDITH—You could not really judge him, all the more because he was not himself at that time.

GEORGETTE—He certainly looked very serious. Do You think he saw the war coming?

EDITH—He says so. What is certain is that from the beginning of that famous week he has been terribly pessimistic, (*silence*).

GEORGETTE—It must seem so extraordinary to him to be here again after those four terrible years.

EDITH—*evasive*—We cannot know what they are going through.

GEORGETTE—Does Paris seem changed to him?

EDITH—I don't think so. Besides, what do you see changed? Some shrapnel holes in the wall of the Ministry of War, there, on the side. Apart from that. . . .

GEORGETTE—As for me, I admit that I still find Paris gloomy. I know that in general no one agrees with me. But it seems that there are many foreigners who are disappointed and who do not want to stay.

EDITH—What do they expect?

GEORGETTE—One can't expect them to understand.

EDITH—Is that so difficult?

GEORGETTE—Among the French who have not been directly hit, how many are there who have truly understood?

EDITH—I do not know what you call "understand."

GEORGETTE—At least those who can imagine . . . , if you wish.

EDITH—One can take the train. I have a friend who went to Reims and returned the same night. She saw. The truth is that those whom you speak of do not want to understand because that would disturb them. They would no longer dare to settle down to their comfortable pre-war life.

GEORGETTE—I think you are unfair; there are some for whom it must require quite an effort. . . .

EDITH—*How indulgent!*

GEORGETTE—Many people think that because of the young they do not have the right to shut themselves in their sorrow. (*with emotion*) As for me, you understand. . . .

EDITH—*in a compassionate tone*—Yes, I know.

GEORGETTE—Basically, what I would like is to live away in the country, to devote my life to a cause. If my mother wanted. . . . For example, all those orphans in the invaded regions.

EDITH—You are very young.

GEORGETTE—If my poor Maurice returned. . . . What does Robert say? Does he think that one can still hope? Tell me sincerely. What's the good of lying!

EDITH—He doesn't know any more than you do. He doesn't even quite know the conditions in which Maurice disappeared.

GEORGETTE—Just the same, he must know if there can still be any secret prisoners.

EDITH—He hasn't heard it mentioned. But how could he affirm anything?

GEORGETTE—When I think that after the war of 1870 hundreds, even thousands remained out there for ten years!

EDITH—We were defeated.

GEORGETTE—Are you really sure that we are the winners? I don't know; I have the impression that they are still very strong and these disturbances, this revolution is just a ruse.

EDITH—You talk like a child.

GEORGETTE—At the Bureau of Missing Persons, they are convinced thet there are still thousands of prisoners in the fortresses, perhaps in Russia. (*silence*) You don't believe that?

EDITH—How could I have an opinion about that?

GEORGETTE—*bitterly*—Basically, you never had any hope. Immediately after, I recall, when the news of the disappearance came to us in Villiers, you were like Maurice's father. Yet, I had so great a need for someone to give me courage.

SCENE TWO

The same, FRANCINE, LISE

LISE—*to Edith*—We come for news. You know that your telephone call the other day could not really satisfy us.

EDITH—That is very kind. You know my sister-in-law, don't you?

GEORGETTE—We met before on the *rue de Hanovre,* when we were bringing back the translated messages.

FRANCINE—Well, how is he?

LISE—He hasn't suffered too much?

FRANCINE—There are not two prisoners who say the same thing.

LISE—They maintain that they have not been mistreated.

FRANCINE—Yet, one reads accounts which make one's flesh crawl. The other day in the newspaper *la Liberté.* . . .

LISE—René says that it must have been exaggerated.

FRANCINE—What does he know about it? . . . (*to Edith*) But what does your husband say?

EDITH—He hasn't said too much up to now.

FRANCINE—Four years! Just think of it! It is dreadful. It is true you must find almost nothing to say to one another . . . , just because too many things have happened. . . .

LISE—Did he receive his packages?

FRANCINE—Ludovic Berthet, my husband's nephew, who comes from there, maintains that the Huns don't lack anything.

LISE—My god-son says just the opposite.

GEORGETTE—We can't know anything. We can't judge.

LISE—But what is your husband's impression of their state of mind? Do they realize that they are defeated?

EDITH—He thinks we signed the armistic too soon. Fifteen days later they would have collapsed.

LISE—That is also what Réne says.

FRANCINE—The high commands have always announced the great victory for the day after. We already saw that in 1915. And on April 16. Léon says that it is an illusion.

LISE—A big offensive was going to be launched in Lorraine, and it seems that there was no opposition. No reserves.

FRANCINE—I doubt it.

GEORGETTE—Just the same it would be dreadful to think that with a little more patience. . . .

FRANCINE—Easily said. Some more victims would have fallen. Now they have been spared. . . .

GEORGETTE—But after so many sacrifices. . . .

FRANCINE—Precisely. Enough of them.

EDITH—My sister-in-law will agree with you in the end.

LISE—What about your husband, madam?

FRANCINE—Did he come back?

GEORGETTE—*indistinctly*—He is a prisoner.

SCENE THREE

The same, ROBERT

LISE—Well, we are very happy to shake your hand. . . . (*she looks at him*). You haven't changed much.

FRANCINE—Perhaps a little thin.

LISE—In the face.

EDITH—Aren't you sorry that we did not wait a little longer to sign the armistice?

ROBERT—I have the impression we were too hasty. (*to Francine*) Is your husband well? Where is he now?

FRANCINE—*with pride*—Captain in the 328th.

LISE—*to Georgette*—Your husband must be eating his heart out. But he should be back soon.

ROBERT—Who must be eating his heart out?

LISE—Your brother, while awaiting his repatriation.

EDITH—*lively*—That's for sure. (*to Robert*) Have you received the card I addressed to you to Copenhagen?

ROBERT—No.

(*In the next room, a child is heard playing one of Beethovens sonatinas very badly*).

LISE—What you must have felt in leaving Germany! And the return to France when you saw the coast!

ROBERT—You know when the time comes, it is always less exalting than one had imagined . . . , if only because one has counted on these joys too much. . . .

GEORGETTE—Well, it must be nice for your family to hear you say that!

ROBERT—You don't understand. I mean to say that an exact account is kept of all we feel. Nothing is omitted, not even what was only anticipation. It is like a loan, you see. Everything you have received beforehand is subtracted from what you will receive in the end.

EDITH—How sad! Then, because so often your heart has beaten faster at the thought of returning. . . . The truth is that you are still very tired. (*to the others*) He came back with a bad stomach.

ROBERT—They stuffed us with food in Denmark.

LISE—Just the same, there is some truth in what you
    say; in general, the people don't seem as happy as
    one would have thought.

ROBERT—There are dishes that one must not allow to
    get cold; any cook will tell you that.

LISE—It is the same with peace.

FRANCINE—What do you think of that Conference?
    They already give the impression of floundering
    pitifully.

LISE—Provided that we do not allow ourselves to be
    done in by our allies.

GEORGETTE—Clemenceau. . . .

LISE—My husband says that he is not the man for the
    job. He would have preferred Briand.

EDITH—But after the Lancken affair. . . .

LISE—People don't seem to know at all what really
    happened.

ROBERT—What is the Lancken affair?

EDITH—I will tell you.

GEORGETTE—This is terrible to say . . . , but don't you
    think that we are going to miss that four o'clock
    bulletin?

EDITH—There are the bulletins of the Conference.

GEORGETTE—No, thanks, they are unreadable. I no
    longer even look at them. Nothing but perpetual
    receptions for delegations and discussions of for-
    malities.

ROBERT—Nevertheless, that is where the destiny of the
    world is decided, at least as much as yesterday on
    the battlefield.

GEORGETTE—It is hard to be convinced of this.

FRANCINE—That's true.

ROBERT—The most exciting bulletins from the Somme
    and Verdun are not nearly as important as the

most trivial of these bulletins that you do not bother to read. We became excited over a piece of terrain, taken, lost, retaken.

LISE—Were you in touch with what was going on while out there?

ROBERT—We got all the bulletins.

FRANCINE—And you managed to size up the situation in spite of all the lies of the German bulletins?

ROBERT—They didn't lie that much. Basically, there was never any real contradiction between their bulletins and ours. I am going to shock you, but it was our bulletins that we suspected the most.

FRANCINE—That's terrible! You were doped by the Huns.

ROBERT—Not at all, but this excess of misleading details only served the purpose of camouflaging the true facts. In September, 1915, for example.

LISE—All the same, that was a great victory.

FRANCINE—Please, don't tell that to my husband who was wounded in front of Sainte-Marie à Py, I know what he told me.

LISE—Each one sees only what's going on in his sector.

EDITH—*to Robert*—But what do you call misleading details?

ROBERT—All those references to numbers, trenches, fortifications, which conceal the brutal fact: we ran smack into the reserve lines which had remained intact.

LISE—We did break through.

FRANCINE—If you call that breaking through! My husband was in the 402nd and it is a miracle that he was not captured.

LISE—Mine was on the staff of the C.O., and he says that if we had not committed an inconceivable error. . . .

FRANCINE—Surely. With some ifs. . . . And what error?

LISE—There is no complete agreement about it. I heard my husband argue about it with one of his friends. As for me, I don't know anything about it. René says that we were taken aback by the casualties.

FRANCINE—It seems to me that there was ample reason for that.

LISE—René says that if we had possessed the courage to make the sacrifice for one big push. . . .

FRANCINE—Why not say "courage to use as gun fodder" while you are at it? "Fodder for this winter," said General Rougé while watching the black troop trains go by. Léon told me about it, these are words one does not easily forget.

LISE—Unfortunately, in war, it is humanitarianism which costs the most. (*to Robert*) You are not saying anything.

ROBERT—I wonder how you lived. Some used to tell us on arriving at the camp: "Women are the most to be pitied."

LISE—That's true.

FRANCINE—It all depends. Many women managed very well during the war, I assure you. The husband or lover on leave became clothed in seductiveness!

ROBERT—I can hardly imagine what it could mean to come thus from the front for eight days.

EDITH—Ten.

LISE—Without counting the day of arrival.

ROBERT—A brief retrieval from horror . . . , and then back to it.

EDITH—Please remind me to give you a short story to read, *The War, Madam,* it is the story of a man on leave.

GEORGETTE—For us all that seems almost incredible already.

LISE—A nightmare.

GEORGETTE—And you will see that it will be forgotten.

FRANCINE—*pointing to Robert*—By them too?

GEORGETTE—They are after all the survivors of war. . . . It is the others whom we should be able to hear. And it is really because the dead keep silent that everything starts all over again.

LISE—It is perhaps better that one doesn't remember too much. It is nature that wishes that great sufferings be forgotten quickly. After all, it will be necessary for us to see them again, to visit them at home.

FRANCINE—We, visit the Huns? Never!

LISE—How could we avoid it? It is not possible.

ROBERT—Well, you will not hold it against us too much if we are bad at helping you remember.

GEORGETTE—Robert, have you jotted down your memoirs, kept a diary?

ROBERT—For what?

GEORGETTE—*with a changed voice*—To preserve it, for everyone to know. All memories vanish. . . . It is dreadful. (*to Edith*) I beg your pardon, my dear. It is late, I should have left long ago. Do not come with me. (*To Edith who has risen in order to accompany her, with a voice shaken by tears*) No, no, do not take the trouble. (*She exits*).

SCENE FOUR

The same, minus GEORGETTE

FRANCINE—Poor woman!

LISE—I beg your pardon; I remembered too late. . . . (*to Robert*) Your brother has disappeared?

ROBERT—Yes, during the attack of May 27.

LISE—But has anyone had news? She said that he was a prisoner.

EDITH—*uneasy*—We have no precise information. My poor sister-in-law wants to hope . . . against all hope.

LISE—How sad! She had a baby, didn't she?

EDITH—It didn't live. (*silence*).

FRANCINE—And she acts as if . . . ? I wouldn't have the courage.

EDITH—Perhaps it isn't courage.

LISE—Each does the best he can. We too must leave. We are expected. (*she rises, as well as Francine*)

EDITH—Thank you. (*she accompanies them*)

SCENE FIVE

EDITH, ROBERT

ROBERT—*very nervous*—Good riddance! These little ladies get on your nerves.

EDITH—I could see they irritated you. Your hands were like that.

ROBERT—What do you expect? I am not always master of myself. Don't you think Suzanne has practised her sonatina enough for today?

EDITH—She has been at the piano for only half an hour. But since that bothers you, I will tell her to stop.

ROBERT—Good, this kind of whining music. . . .

EDITH—It is Beethoven.

ROBERT—But what a Beethoven! And how played! Oh! I am willing to admit that a child of nine. . . .

EDITH—I am going to tell her to stop and I'm coming back. (*She leaves. Robert goes to the window and whistles, his hands in his pockets*).

EDITH—*re-entering*—There. You'll have peace.

ROBERT—Good. Now, tell me why does Georgette adopt this attitude? She cannot be deceiving herself!

EDITH—I know nothing about it. I refrain from speaking with her too much.

ROBERT—They told us out there that there were some people in France who thought . . . , but I thought that it was people in a completely different milieu. As for me, it has been months since I have given up all hopes for Maurice. When you wrote me: "He is listed as disappeared." . . . And on top of that you told me about the report made by a wounded man from his company. . . .

EDITH—*tense*—Georgette doesn't know it.

ROBERT—But then, why haven't you informed her?

EDITH—What are you saying? What do you expect? I didn't have the courage.

ROBERT—Well, you have done the greatest wrong. She is torturing herself. I am convinced that she broke down after leaving. There is nothing worse than this uncertainty. Truth always calms in the long run.

EDITH—Permit me to disagree. If there is one field in which one can't generalize. . . . You know that I did work in connection with missing soldiers.

ROBERT—That was a queer idea! There were so many other things you could have done instead.

EDITH—Anyhow, there are many people who would much rather not know.

ROBERT—*pursuing his thought*—A streak of compassion, I suppose.

EDITH—*disconcerted*—What? Oh! Robert, how can you?

ROBERT—I don't know. I am trying to understand. You had the children to take care of. And you could have knitted socks, rolled bandages, and what not!

EDITH—It seems at times that you are deliberately trying to hurt me. For example, just a few minutes ago, what you said about your return. What must they have thought?

ROBERT—If that is all that worries you, it is not serious.

EDITH—It was heartless! You admit. . . .

ROBERT—What do you expect? I am not really feeling up to the mark. I just went to see Dr. Perrinier.

EDITH—Why without me?

ROBERT—I preferred to be alone with him. Women make a tragedy of everything.

EDITH—*with tears in her eyes*—Robert, am I like that?

ROBERT—Sorry, dear.

EDITH—What did he say?

ROBERT—Well, decidedly I have a bad stomach. He made out a new prescription for me. I told him that the drug he gave me the other day had no effect on me, one way or another.

EDITH—You have hardly given it a try. Four days!

ROBERT—You think so? Yes, in fact, you are right.

EDITH—Well, what are you going to do?

ROBERT—I am going to mix them both.

EDITH—You are ridiculous.

ROBERT—He spoke to me about our little boy. I didn't know that his enteritis had been so serious. In short, I was not kept informed of anything.

EDITH—You reproach me for not wanting to give you cause for worry?

ROBERT—Not a question of reproach. I state the fact. Basically. . . .

EDITH—What?

ROBERT—*abruptly*—You find me changed, don't you? Yes, a little thin, I know. But that is not what I am asking you.

EDITH—You are a little irritable; that is perfectly natural after all you've gone through.

ROBERT—We did not suffer that much. Besides, the poor fellows in the trenches. . . . And you know I would perhaps have been a poor combattant. The first time I saw fire in Hautmont. . . .

EDITH—I know. What does that prove?

ROBERT—Evidently it doesn't prove anything. You have a way of saying things. But people badly need to believe in our past suffering in order to bear with us today. It is a bit painful to feel oneself excused to this extent. . . .

EDITH—I don't understand. Excused? A whole lot of you were made prisoners together.

ROBERT—There are men in my regiment who found a way to escape. And then out there in the prison camp, after all . . . , I could still have escaped.

EDITH—From the middle of Silesia! Robert!

ROBERT—Bad luck I wasn't in the Rhineland, eh? But, after all, some managed to get to Bohemia. (*silence*).

SCENE SIX

The same, MRS. LECHEVALLIER, GUSTAVE

ROBERT—Good morning, mother. Hello, Gustave!

MRS. LECHEVALLIER—Your brother came to surprise us after lunch.

GUSTAVE—I am here for twenty-four hours.

MRS. LECHEVALLIER—Poor Georgette just left my house in such a state. . . . I am still upset from it. She should not even have. . . . But she does not realize. Poor girl! One cannot expect her to have considerations. . . .

EDITH—What did she say to you?

MRS. LECHEVALLIER—I don't exactly know what put her in that mood. (*to Robert*) It is what you said just a moment ago while she spoke of Maurice. She suspected that you knew more.

ROBERT—I?

EDITH—And she asked you to ask him the question?

MRS. LECHEVALLIER—No. But she scared me. I thought that perhaps she was right and that you were concealing from us a bad piece of news.

ROBERT—Poor mother. . . . But I will be completely honest. It is clear that we should not have any illusions about Maurice. Just think! The armistice was signed on November 11.

MRS. LECHEVALLIER—But I am given to understand that there are still soldiers who cannot be repatriated. And after all, as long as we don't know anything for sure. . . .

ROBERT—*to Edith*—But, Edith. . . .

MRS. LECHEVALLIER—Two days ago, near my home, a man who was never able to write to his family came back.

ROBERT—Do you know his name and military address?

MRS. LECHEVALLIER—I can find out.

GUSTAVE—*sententiously*—It is certain that there is only a very slim chance. However, one must not despair, and so long as we do not have any definite report. . . .

ROBERT—Edith, I don't understand you. . . . To keep alive this hope in poor mother doesn't make sense.

MRS. LECHEVALLIER—You break my heart. Georgette was right. You are inhuman. And when I recall. . . .

ROBERT—What, mother?

MRS. LECHEVALLIER—He loved you so much, pitied

you. . . . Edith, you remember when, on furlough, in the garden in Chavançon he stopped and said, "Poor Robert! Confined behind barbed wire!" How he pitied you! He said, "As for me, I could not endure such an existence. Fortunately he is more courageous than I." (*she cries*).

GUSTAVE—Come now, mother. Don't get overwrought.

MRS. LECHEVALLIER—And when he heard that you were retaliated against, do you recall his letter, Edith? "Those bandits," he said, "I want to kill them, to kill them. . . ." He was afraid that you would not come back. I don't know what he would have done, had you died out there.

ROBERT—Poor mother! What would you have had him do?

MRS. LECHEVALLIER—And you defend them!

ROBERT—Am I defending them?

MRS. LECHEVALLIER—They have killed your brother and you defend them! Yesterday evening. . . .

ROBERT—What did I say? Oh! with regard to the questioning! Nevertheless it is only too certain that we acted just as they did and that we employed every means to make the prisoners talk. . . . Not always, but often.

MRS. LECHEVALLIER—That's fine! You put us in the same class as those monsters.

EDITH—Mother, if you would come and say hello! to the children, it would calm you down a bit, I'm sure.

MRS. LECHEVALLIER—You're right. At least they will not do me any harm, not they.

SCENE SEVEN

ROBERT, GUSTAVE, *then* EDITH

ROBERT—Poor mother is high strung.

GUSTAVE—Especially since the alerts.

ROBERT—But she left immediately for Villiers.

GUSTAVE—She was here during the first days when the "Big Bertha" gun was placed in position—and even after that; she worried about me. You know that the Ministry of War was one of the main targets. And then the disappearance of Maurice! You do not seem to understand enough that one must weigh one's words. You are back in a country which is just recovering from an illness.

ROBERT—*curtly*—Thanks. (*the sonatina can be heard again from the next room*) Good gracious! That concert is starting again. The country seems to be having a rather joyous convalescence.

GUSTAVE—What do you expect? Life must begin again. If only from the economic point of view. That doesn't put a stop to thinking and suffering.

EDITH—*re-entering*—There. Mother evidently preferred to stay alone with them. (*They hear Mrs. Lechevallier who counts out loud: one, two, three, four; not so fast, Suzanne*).

GUSTAVE—There is one thing you have to learn. That applies to all of you, unavoidably.

ROBERT—Who is that "you"?

GUSTAVE—All those who return from Germany. Here, we have passed through such anxieties. . . . For my part, I assure you I no longer recognize myself.

ROBERT—As for me, I recognize you very well.

GUSTAVE—You believe it, but you will see gradually

how much I have changed. We have known very anxious moments, on the Boulevard Saint-Germain! You just can't imagine. Take, for example, March 21, when we knew that they had broken through. I had to run to G.H.Q. No, you cannot imagine the state in which we were. For you, all that must have lost some of its sting. While here! you will agree, we were in the very heart of the drama. There have been times when I envied the men in the trenches, I assure you. They saw only their sector, they didn't panic; whereas the rest of us here, we knew the sorry lot who came back from Russia.

ROBERT—We suspected as much, you know.

GUSTAVE—Yes, but you didn't know how few combat troops we had at our disposal. Well trained men. Naturally, I don't mean that it was fun for the rest of you, but . . . you at least didn't have any responsibilities.

ROBERT—Then, your ideal is not to have any?

GUSTAVE—*without listening*—It is frightening, you know. . . .

ROBERT—Did you have such heavy responsibilities? I did not have any idea of it.

GUSTAVE—Many more than you think, old chap. There are many things that will become known later only.

ROBERT—*standing at the far end*—I thought that you were only a transmission agent.

GUSTAVE—There are many methods of transmitting, you know, and I recall certain conversations with Chantilly. . . .

ROBERT—Who is in this picture? Is it Maurice?

EDITH—It had been taken by one of his friends during his last furlough.

GUSTAVE—Three weeks before he disappeared.

ROBERT—I had difficulty in recognizing him. Did the war change him that much? Did it make of him this splendid fellow?

EDITH—Didn't anyone ever think of sending you any photographs of Maurice?

ROBERT—They must have feared that the Huns would confiscate them. But I can't get over it. He looked like a warrior in the photograph. I recall the puny person he used to be! Even the look is no longer the same: so much more assured. He who always looked evasive and a little sad. This is a face which breathes . . . a kind of liveliness.

EDITH—*seriously*—Maurice was happy in the army.

GUSTAVE—It must be said that he had some first-rate comrades and an outstanding commander.

EDITH—Except during the atrocious periods, especially at Verdun and perhaps at the Somme, he didn't stop congratulating himself on his luck.

ROBERT—Are you sure?

EDITH—I am sure of it.

ROBERT—I couldn't have the faintest idea of what was happening, since we were not allowed to correspond. Mother and you, you both wrote to me: "Maurice is well . . ." "Maurice has just been decorated . . ." "Maurice has been slightly wounded —a matter of a few weeks." What do such things tell you about someone's life?

GUSTAVE—Edith is right. Not only has Maurice acted with great dignity, but he was lucky up to that damned incident of last May.

ROBERT—Would one ever have suspected it? He was actually the least militaristic of us three. . . . You cannot have received many letters from him. He has always been a bad correspondent. I am not talking of those which his wife may have received.

EDITH—*simply*—Maurice wrote to me a lot.

ROBERT—*stupefied*—To you?

EDITH—He often had some advice to give me for Georgette, . . . especially during her pregnancy.

ROBERT—Yes, but except for that. . . .

GUSTAVE—*pulling out his watch*—I am going to tell mother that if she stays any longer, I will not be able to wait for her. (*he leaves*).

SCENE EIGHT

ROBERT, EDITH

ROBERT—"Except for what"?

EDITH—*in a constrained voice*—Maurice didn't want to give his wife any details for fear of upsetting her. It was to me and to his mother that he wrote at length, especially to me, of course.

ROBERT—Of course? . . . Will you show me those letters?

EDITH—I will show you some of them, if you insist.

ROBERT—Why not all?

EDITH—All are not . . . interesting, and then there are some which I don't feel I have the right to show you.

ROBERT—What a joke!

EDITH—It is very serious, believe me.

ROBERT—But since the poor boy spoke of me with so much affection. . . .

EDITH—That's no reason. You. . . . (*she breaks off*).

ROBERT—Well?

EDITH—I find that you did not always speak of Maurice as you should have. You made fun of him in the past, and the memory of these jokes is painful to me. . . . Even now you do not seem to have for him . . . , for his memory . . . , the respect which is fitting.

ROBERT—What has come over you?

EDITH—When I think of what these years have been for him, and of that horrible death so little time before the end of the nightmare. . . . The idea that in the past. . . .

ROBERT—That's childish. Could I foresee that he would become . . . a hero?

EDITH—Not that word, not that tone, if you please. . . . Yes, we should have suspected it.

ROBERT—What an excitement! (*silence*).

EDITH—Positively I will not show you those letters. You have a talent for tearing down people and that is something I would not put up with. It is too bad that you didn't know Maurice, the real Maurice, but. . . .

ROBERT—What if those letters really permit me to get a glimpse of him!

EDITH—The risk is too great.

ROBERT—What risk?

EDITH—I repeat; I could not forgive you for making certain remarks. And you cannot guarantee me that they will not escape you. You have too little control over yourself. I know, it is not your fault, and it is not a question of blaming you for it. . . . Gustave's lack of sensitivity makes me furious.

ROBERT—He is so utterly stupid. On that matter, at least, everyone agrees.

EDITH—*after a slight pause*—I beg your pardon, Robert. . . .

ROBERT—For what?

EDITH—You must regain a taste for life, for our life. It is only then that we can ask you to be just. . . . Until then you have every right.

ROBERT—Except the one to read Maurice's letters. Obviously, you are making a real effort to recall constantly the sufferings which I am supposed to have undergone. You cling to them as to a rock so as not to fall . . . It is intolerable.

EDITH—Oh! no, I do not make any such effort.

ROBERT—Yes, you do, it is as if you press a button when you feel that you are getting too mad at me.

SCENE NINE

The same, MRS. LECHEVALLIER

MRS. LECHEVALLIER—I have just passed a few nice minutes with the children. Suzanne already plays very nicely, but she doesn't know the divisions. As for Jimmy, he is a darling; and Loulou. . . .

ROBERT—*exasperated*—Oh! no, not Loulou, please; his name is Louis.

MRS. LECHEVALLIER—Everybody has always called him Loulou. It is a habit one develops, that's all.

ROBERT—No. That will have to change.

MRS. LECHEVALLIER—What a dictator!

EDITH—You know that I too don't like those nicknames very much.

MRS. LECHEVALLIER—Louis! It sounds like an accountant. (*to Robert*) I'd like you to know that you scare him.

ROBERT—Nonsense.

MRS. LECHEVALLIER—Irma is sure of it; and yesterday at lunch I noticed it. You must be careful. There are impressions that penetrate more deeply than one thinks. For example, I recall that aunt Séraphine. . . . What could I give Loulou for his birthday, Edith?

EDITH—*to Robert*—Remember that he will be five the day after tomorrow.

MRS. LECHEVALLIER—I shall give him a present on behalf of Maurice. (*with emotion*). Maurice loved him so much! He had transferred to him . . . (*to Edith*) Do the little ones speak of him sometimes?

EDITH—Often, especially Jimmy.

MRS. LECHEVALLIER—You can't imagine what he meant for them. On each of his furloughs he looked after them as if he was their father. . . . When he insisted on taking Suzanne to the oculist. . . .

EDITH—That was overly exaggerated. But he felt responsible, that's for sure.

MRS. LECHEVALLIER—The walks that he took with them during his furloughs! They were so gay!

ROBERT—Maurice gay? Definitely. . . .

MRS. LECHEVALLIER—He was so cut out for family life! When the baby died, I do not hesitate to say that he was sadder than Georgette.

EDITH—This only shows she was exhausted, sick. . . . In such cases, one no longer feels anything.

MRS. LECHEVALLIER—You remember what he wrote before the birth. Those instructions for everything. He wished so much that Georgette would be able to nurse her child. In fact he was wrong. With her health! . . . and the name he chose! (*to Robert*) He sent a telegram that they should add Robert to the names André François.

ROBERT—I didn't know.

MRS. LECHEVALLIER—Didn't you write that to him?

EDITH—Of course, I did. Didn't I hear the bell?

Mrs. Lechevallier—Perhaps it is Father Séveilhac.

Edith—What is he doing here?

Mrs. Lechevallier—He wrote to me that he would come to see us, and he would like to meet Robert.

Robert—Who is he?

Edith—The chaplain of Maurice's battalion. I told you about him, I remember.

Mrs. Lechevallier—He is a saint.

Edith—Do not say that, mother; you are going to make him look ridiculous in Robert's eyes.

SCENE TEN

The same, Father Séveilhac
(Dressed as military chaplain, highly decorated, very strong southern accent)

Fr. Séveilhac—Good morning, madam.

Edith—*in a subdued voice*—What a pity you were not able to let me know ahead of time, Father! May I introduce my husband. . . . I am sure we are going to be disturbed. I who would have liked so much to speak to you undisturbed. At least you will stay for dinner. Yes, yes, you must.

Mrs. Lechevallier—In any case, I will not be the one to disturb you; I must go.

Edith—Look, mother, I didn't say that for you. (*she sees her to the door*)

Robert—*to the priest*—I know that you knew my brother Maurice very well, Father.

Fr. Séveilhac—Intimately. . . . For more than three years I saw him everyday, and his disappearance caused me the greatest grief.

Edith—*re-entering with the three children*—Come on, come and say hello! to Father.

Fr. Séveilhac—Oh! madam, but how they have

changed! (*to Louis*) I am sure he does not recognize me. He was still so little when I saw him the last time. You recall, madam, when I passed through Chavançon? It must have been more than a year ago.

EDITH—Yes, at the time of my brother-in-law's furlough.

FR. SÉVEILHAC—*to Robert, pointing to James*—How this one resembles you! He has exactly your forehead. This little girl takes more after her mother. She has your beautiful dark eyes, madam.

ROBERT—*evidently irritated*—Say, Edith, the children haven't been out today. Would you mind if I took them out for a walk?

SUZANNE—Oh! mother! I would have like to stay with Father.

FR. SÉVEILHAC—Now, now!

LITTLE LOUIS—*pointing to the priest's cross*—It is like my uncle Maurice's.

FR. SÉVEILHAC—My, what a memory!

ROBERT—Let's go!

EDITH—Don't tire them too much. You walk too fast.

ROBERT—I assure you I no longer have my former stride. You need not be concerned.

SCENE ELEVEN

EDITH, FR. SÉVEILHAC

EDITH—It is good to see you, Father, very good. . . . I have not seen you since September, when you were merely passing through.

FR. SÉVEILHAC—In that blasted railroad station of Lyons, there was no chance to chat. We could not hear one another.

EDITH—I had so many things to tell you. . . .

FR. SÉVEILHAC—Your letters have kept me partly informed. You told me about that repatriated man who witnessed the captain's last hours. And poor Georgette, how is she? How did she hold up under that blow?

EDITH—I haven't told her anything, Father, . . . and I would very much like you to tell me why.

FR. SÉVEILHAC—What's that what you are asking me now? Were you afraid of causing her pain?

EDITH—Perhaps she would suffer less if she knew the truth. No, I know it is much more complicated than that.

FR. SÉVEILHAC—It is you who are so complicated, madam. I told you that already in Chavançon.

EDITH—It is not entirely my fault, Father.

FR. SÉVEILHAC—I don't know. I think these complications do not displease you. They have helped you to pass the time. . . . Nowadays, madam, women have too much leisure. They keep their hands busy with embroidering, with sewing, or even . . . ; but during that time, the mind works too; it builds and it distorts! (*he smacks his tongue against his teeth*). One should learn not to think, you see. There is a certain peace of mind which is necessary for the health of the soul. From your expression I can sense that you are going to tell me some dreadful things. I read it in your face.

EDITH—*in a low voice*—I am suffering.

FR. SÉVEILHAC—I am sure that you are not diligent enough in your religious exercises. I know that what I am saying to you sounds pretty stupid. But you see, for a woman like you, a woman who thinks too much, those exercises are very important.

EDITH—Because they put a stop to thinking.

Fr. Séveilhac—You know well that it is not so, but, if you wish, you may say that they channel your thought. Do not say that they reduce it to a mere mechanism.

Edith—*with a sad smile*—I say nothing.

Fr. Séveilhac—There is a danger in a thought that is too free, a thought that capers. . . .

Edith—Mine doesn't caper, Father.

Fr. Séveilhac—Which capers, with the bridle on the neck, like a colt in the meadow. It is a little humiliating for us, I know . . . , I have devoted much time to understanding what I am telling you. I believe that it is Pascal who made it clear to me . . . , and also that terrible life out there on the battle field. Even to pray mechanically has its value, I assure you.

Edith—I want to believe you, Father, although I do not understand it very well.

Fr. Séveilhac—It is the only way for us to remember that we are souls . . . when the beast is very tired or when it is naughty and cries too loud. . . . Your poor brother-in-law knew it well. I remember one evening, near Cléry, we knew that the battalion had to attack at night. . . . (*he does not finish*). Why do you look at me that way?

Edith—Father, I suffer. . . . And when I don't suffer it is still worse. . . . Tell me, you never answered a question I asked you in one of my letters, it must have been nearly two months ago.

Fr. Séveilhac—*simply*—That's true, I didn't want to answer you.

Edith—Do you remember exactly what I asked you?

Fr. Séveilhac—Yes.

Edith—And you could have answered me?

Fr. Séveilhac—*with a kind of indignation*—You must

be out of your mind! Do you think that I am going
to repeat to you what your brother-in-law confided
to me?

EDITH—Thus, you deny me the right to try to understand what he thought during those last weeks.

FR. SÉVEILHAC—By admitting even for an instant that
a sinful love had sprouted in this hero's
breast. . . .

EDITH—Please, no more of those big words which cut
one down to size.

FR. SÉVEILHAC—I said, "By admitting"—you do not
have to know it. You should be the first to refrain
from thinking such a thing. He loved you like a
brother and he gave you repeated proofs of it. . . .

EDITH—You don't understand. It is not a question of
knowing if he felt for me what you call a sinful
love; it is a question of knowing if he loved me,
that's all. Father, remember that we are speaking
of a dead person, and there can no longer be
anything impure in what he inspires in me.

FR. SÉVEILHAC—*with sadness*—You believe that; but as
for me, I am not convinced of it. One speaks only
of the living, and it is actually about the living that
you are questioning me. One prays for the dead;
that is altogether a different matter.

EDITH—I can't say to what extent your words chill me.
. . . It seems that this prayer to which you invite
me exiles to infinity those for whom it is offered;
between them and us, it puts more than space, it
puts God himself. One can only pray for those
who are truly absent, . . . but you can't pretend
that death is an absence! There are times, Father,
when he is more immediately present to me than
he ever was in life. No longer is there between him

and me this dreadful fear of thinking of one another in a sinful way; no longer is there the disturbing image of third parties. . . . There are no longer
any third parties. Don't give me that harsh look,
Father; I see too clearly that you don't grasp. And
yet, you should remember, you should understand. . . .

Fr. Séveilhac—I know that your brother-in-law was
very good; I know he was goodness itself. You have
the right, the duty, I admit, of preserving for him a
deep gratitude for the way in which he fulfilled the
fraternal obligations which the absence of your
husband created for him.

Edith—But now that his substitution has ended. . . .
Father, why do you speak of all that as of dead
things? What are these offensive words concerning
obligations and gratitude doing here? And to what
guilty passion do you oppose the decent sentiments, the thankful and normal affection that he
should inspire in me? All that is wrong, all that is
outside what I feel and live.

Fr. Séveilhac—Basically, it is not quite simply—you
will not mind my telling you my thoughts
frankly?—that these too long awaited reunions are
disturbing and begin by deceiving.

Edith—*in a muffled voice*—This feeling of absence that
a dead loved one could not awaken in us I experience for my husband with a horrible intensity. . . .
He is always at a distance—and that is not saying
enough, for space itself does not separate those
who worship one another. He is not with me, we
are not together; we are . . . , I don't know how to
explain to you, . . . let us say, like objects placed
near one another, forever outside one another. And

yet, if only you knew how passionately I desired that it be otherwise.

FR. SÉVEILHAC—But formerly, before the war. . . .

EDITH—We were a good couple, yes, Father. So what? And then, what does this word itself mean exactly? That there was never between us any quarrel that one can recall, that one can relate. When I think of those years, my thought sinks into darkness. . . . My husband was very much absorbed in his business. My two older children have been difficult to raise; as for myself, I was very sick after Jacques' birth. . . . This is what my life was made up of. What would become of us without all those accidents that irritate us? They are necessary to fill our poor existence. Without that. . . .

FR. SÉVEILHAC—Madam Edith, you frighten me.

EDITH—At times, I am frightened to see myself so lucid.

FR. SÉVEILHAC—These are perhaps the times when you are most completely mistaken about yourself and others. But, instead of becoming wrapt up in yourself, if you thought more about your husband, about what those four frightening years have been. . . . Even if they have changed his personality a little, isn't that natural?

EDITH—If you knew how I make allowance for him! I make too many allowances for him. When one excuses so easily, it is really the best proof that one does not. . . .

FR. SÉVEILHAC—What else are you going to say? Madam Edith, I do not want to hear such things.

EDITH—Won't you permit me to confess to you?

FR. SÉVEILHAC—That is not a confession. By repeating certain phrases, one ends up by thinking them. There are words one must not use. . . . And then, besides, what does all that mean? There is only one thing that counts, and that is your duty, which is perfectly clear. With all your strength, you must apply yourself to drive away these ideas. They are fatal, they are deadly. . . . You tell me that this feeling you experience is not sinful; would you admit it to your husband?

EDITH—*clearly*—I have thought about it very seriously. It is possible that I may end up doing that.

FR. SÉVEILHAC—*strongly*—You would be most wrong.

EDITH—And how?

FR. SÉVEILHAC—You would be most wrong. You would make your husband unhappy and you would still strengthen this obsession within yourself. There is nothing outside which can respond to this feeling. It is within your power not to let it spread, not to let it grip you like a fever, or on the contrary to let it die out slowly. I know what you are going to answer: you cling to that feeling, you don't want it to die, you surrender to it with a kind of secret delight. Isn't that concupiscence?

EDITH—I won't ever tell you that, Father. You tell me that nothing outside can respond to my feeling. I don't know what you mean by that. Or rather yes, I think I know. (*with sobs in her throat*) Basically, for you, the dead are no longer there; and your thoughts are in no way different from those who do not believe. Whatever be the glorious and unimaginable existence that you ascribe to them . . . , for you they are no longer of the living. But for me . . . the truly dead, the only dead are those whom we no longer love.

FR. SÉVEILHAC—And his wife . . . , would you confide this to her?

EDITH—I know that she would not understand me. She

would pretend to keep him all to herself, as if in that world there were still parts, as if there were still privileges!

FR. SÉVEILHAC—By what right do you deny her the supreme wisdom that you claim for yourself?

EDITH—Maybe because we did not belong to each other on earth that it was given to me to understand so clearly. . . .

FR. SÉVEILHAC—You are a mystic, madam Edith!

EDITH—What is there in that thought that you scorn?

FR. SÉVEILHAC—And you are proud of it.

EDITH—You are trying to locate me somewhere in your experience: one would say that you are trying to get my bearings as one does for a boat.

FR. SÉVEILHAC—But how you express yourself! I can see that you are very much accustomed to reasoning on all those difficult and dangerous things.

EDITH—Don't attribute any virtuosity to me please, Father. One doesn't know how complicated nature can become. Reasoning works only in a crude way. . . .

FR. SÉVEILHAC—In all that you have said, there is not a word which becomes a Christian.

EDITH—Does it depend on me to have an orthodox heart?

FR. SÉVEILHAC—Do you claim that the will armed with faith is powerless against an evil such as that which undermines you?

EDITH—It seems to me that what you raise up before me is lifeless ghosts.

FR. SÉVEILHAC—Religion, a ghost!

EDITH—The religion that you put before me is none other than an ethic; pardon me for saying that my whole being abhors this ethic. The only religion that can count for me is that which introduces us to another world, in which the miserable barriers that separate incarnate beings vanish in love and in charity. Yes, we are intimately united, he and I; yes, I feel he is with me, ever closer to me. And I revolt against the idea that this can be sinful. For that is life, and all the rest in my eyes is only. . . .

FR. SÉVEILHAC—The rest, what you call the rest, is trial. Whatever the bonds that unite beings in the other life . . . , for us who are still engaged in the struggle, the danger is fatal for anyone who wants to have right now this promised happiness. (*with brutality*) You are exposed to all kinds of superstition.

EDITH—I can't think like you. . . . Don't brandish your dogma in order to strike me down, Father. . . . You speak of trial, election, danger. Is it therefore by the narrow gate of competition that one gets to heaven? Is it really meriting that is important? The faith to which you were vainly summoning me a few minutes ago, the faith that is beyond coercion and clings to the bottom of my soul revolts against this very thought. If it is enough to merit, if it is merit that counts, well then, it is that instructor at Chavançon who is right. . . . and then it is not worth believing in God.

FR. SÉVEILHAC—Madam Edith, don't you feel the monstrous immorality of. . . .

EDITH—You speak to me of superstition; you accuse me of immorality. . . . I am so certain that you don't understand me. And yet, you have seen so many die in your arms. . . . How is it that your thought did not yearn to follow their path beyond what one can see or hear. . . . How did you resign yourself? . . .

FR. SÉVEILHAC—I have faith in the God of mercy who

has received these souls in order to save them.

EDITH—*with vigor*—It is enough for you to have made over to Him . . . this sacred trust; once this task is accomplished, you wash your hands of it. When the dying have taken their final breath, there remains for you I know not what satisfaction of a conscientious functionary who rubs his hands, his day's work done, in front of the accumulated piles of papers. . . . But to live with them, to draw from them the inspiration which comforts and sustains, that, you say, is superstition; it is. . . . (*she bursts into tears*).

FR. SÉVEILHAC—*with sudden softness*—Pardon me, madam Edith. . . . I realize that I have spoken to you brutally. It is because I was afraid for you.

EDITH—*with irony*—For my soul?

FR. SÉVEILHAC—Tell me: did you think that you had communication with your brother-in-law?

EDITH—What are you supposing? Do you imagine me during lonely evenings with my hands on a table?

FR. SÉVEILHAC—This would not be more dangerous . . . , it would not even be more ridiculous. (*Edith is startled*)

EDITH—When I think of him in a certain way—with tenderness, with recollection—there wells up in me something like a richer, deeper life in which I know he participates. This life is not I, nor is it he; it is both of us. Shall I admit it to you? I was hoping a little that you would be able to take part in this kind of conversation without words, the sweetness of which. . . . (*with emotion*). Why does it seem to me now that I am violating a sacred prohibition by telling you that? It is something about which one must not speak (*sternly*) with a stranger. In reality, I have betrayed him.

SCENE TWELVE

The same, ROBERT

(Robert makes a motion of astonishment which he does not bother to hide while seeing the priest).

EDITH—It seems that you were gone a long time.

ROBERT—Indeed.

EDITH—Aren't the children tired? . . . You are pale.

ROBERT—You know I am no longer used to walking.

FR. SÉVEILHAC—Those cruel years of captivity really must have tested you physically and morally. Oh! doubtless you would not agree with that. I know you are brave. Your brother told me about you. So you are not a stranger to me.

ROBERT—It is possible that my brother was mistaken about me, as, it seems, I have been about him.

FR. SÉVEILHAC—*surprised*—Really?

ROBERT—There is nothing in all they tell me about him which corresponds to my memories.

FR. SÉVEILHAC—I think that in the past he was scared of you; he had such a mistrust of himself.

ROBERT—That still is for me a true revelation. And, you see, Father, all these belated findings are painful to me, so much so that I would beg you to be so kind as to spare me the news. I imagine that my wife feels a kind of satisfaction in conversing with you about a person whom she has, it seems, known perfectly; but as for me. . . .

FR. SÉVEILHAC—*getting up*—I understand you very well. Besides, I have stayed too long.

ROBERT—But, Father, there are other topics of conversation.

FR. SÉVEILHAC—*without answering, to Edith*—Goodbye

madam. (*Edith rises to accompany him to the door*)

Robert—Never mind. It is up to me to see Father to the door.

SCENE THIRTEEN

Edith, Robert

Robert—At last! . . . But what! Tell me, did Maurice also become a bigot?

Edith—*bitterly*—Maurice was very religious during those last years, that is certain.

Robert—And did he communicate to you a little of this fervor? I can't imagine you five years ago keeping up a conversation for one hour and a half with a priest, and what a conversation! When I walked in again, I thought I saw. . . .

Edith—Are you truly convinced about knowing so clearly my previous thoughts, those of five years ago?

Robert—I beg you, don't assume those mysterious airs. I assure you that I feel very unwilling to tolerate them. The war may have changed many things; it has certainly not altered my memory, and I have kept a very clear image of what you were . . . before this nightmare.

Edith—The image . . . of my physical person perhaps. But . . . what about the rest, Robert? I don't think that you can have an image of that.

Robert—*with a kind of despair*—Upon my word, one would say that you are all trying to create a vacuum around me. . . . I don't know if you are doing that so as to make me think of myself as a ghost.

EDITH—*with commiseration*—Listen to me, Robert.

ROBERT—No. Above all spare me the explanations. If you show me that I am wrong, you will only aggravate me more. And if you agree that I am right, . . . I know too well that this will be a concession made out of pity. I prefer your cruel mouth and your silence.

EDITH—*sadly*—Then it is better that I leave. (*She goes slowly to the door, but just as she turns the doorknob . . .*)

ROBERT—*sharply*—Do you think that things are going to be like this for ever? Tell me, for if so, then it would be enough to make me run away; or else, I don't know, I. . . .

EDITH—But think! If you did not persist in interpreting everything that I say or don't say to you, if you took my words as they come. . . .

ROBERT—When one has too long, too obstinately thought of someone, Edith, and when one sees him again, one must spell out anew all his words and all his gestures. Because one is accustomed to remember him saying other words, making other gestures. . . . I know that you don't understand. Don't bother.

EDITH—But of course, my dear, I want to understand, and I will understand.

ROBERT—And then, when one finds that the person changed . . . and especially changing, unstable, impenetrable.

EDITH—We miss the cliché.

ROBERT—No, not even that. The cliché has disappeared. The cliché was good while waiting. . . . But whenever there is no longer anything to wait for. . . .

EDITH—*sorrowfully*—Poor Robert!

SCENE FOURTEEN

The same, SOLANGE, *The maid*

EDITH—What is it Solange?

SOLANGE—A telegram for madam. (*she leaves*)

EDITH—*looking*—Constantine. It is from aunt Helen. (*reading*) "So happy to know Robert was repatriated. We wholeheartedly join in your happiness."